CREATE-IT COUNSELING

By Paula Cox, Ph.D., NCSC

Grades 3-8

44 Hands-On, Experiential-Based Lessons to Engage Students

* Bullying & Relational Issues
* Self-Regulation
* Resiliency Revolution
* Identity Formation

youth light inc.

© 2015 by YouthLight, Inc.
Chapin, SC 29036

Cover Design by Amy Rule
Layout by Diane Florence
Project Editing by Susan Bowman

ISBN
978-1-59850-175-9

Library of Congress Number
2015931446

10 9 8 7 6 5 4 3 2 1
Printed in the United States

Acknowledgements and Dedication

*I would like to thank my family and friends
for their constant love, support, and encouragement.
Thanks for helping me live a more meaningful life.*

Table of Contents

Table of Contents

Introduction

Welcome to the user guide section of this book! This section will help the user understand the concept behind incorporating creative activities into individual, group, and classroom sessions. Tips are given to ensure that you and your students have a great experience learning ideas and principles to live a more meaningful life!

About This Book

Have you ever wondered how to make counseling more concrete or experience-oriented? Or maybe you have a few students that seem to be disengaged. The goal of **Create-It Counseling** is to equip helping professionals with hands-on activities and experience-oriented session ideas that teach or reinforce therapeutic concepts.

Incorporating the use of creative activities makes for memorable moments of learning for students of all ages. These experiences and moments of creating help ensure skill transference to environments outside of the counseling office or classroom. And as an added bonus, during many of the sessions, students create visual art or reminders that they can take home or to the classroom!

The vision for this book came after two mediocre classroom guidance lessons. I had recently changed positions from being a traditional school counselor to working with the district's population of students that had high rates of discipline referrals and trips to the Juvenile Detention Center. After the second attempt of classroom guidance, I knew they were not really invested and probably were not even giving a second thought to the lesson presented once I left. So, I came up with a plan...a different plan--that involved less talking and more creating and interaction. As the students entered the room, there was immediate interest. "What is that stuff for?" "What are we doing?" "I am not making anything!"

Needless to say, at the end of our first session called, *The Blob*, all of my students were working together, manipulating their slime creations and making all kinds of inferences about their life and choices. They even wanted a group picture taken! And the best part, when I returned the next time, I heard stories about what happened when they got home and how they had made some different choices during the week that helped their situations be a little less messy! Success!

I hope as you use this book your students become engaged and more importantly, are empowered to make choices that make their worlds a little better! What are you waiting for? Go grab some supplies and start **Create-It Counseling**!

Rationale

Engaging students in today's fast-paced, instant download society can often be a challenge. Current educational trends and techniques encourage teaching methodology that incorporates hands-on activities. The experience oriented activities seek to assist students in understanding and applying techniques instead of memorizing steps and procedures. For example, instead of just lecturing about geometric shapes and students memorizing how many sides each has, students may be asked to create models of geometric shapes and present charts documenting common uses of the shapes. Many classrooms today have the appearance of exploratory labs instead of lecture rooms. The underlying rationale is that students are more likely to engage and understand concepts when they actually "experience" learning.

So, is the incorporation and emphasis on experience oriented or creative techniques a new idea in the counseling world? Absolutely not. Using such activities and the arts to help people deal with stress and life issues finds its origins as far back as ancient society (Waliski, 2009). The use of music, drama, and visual art were all avenues used to help people cope with difficult issues or to demonstrate a virtue or cultural lesson. According to Gladding (2011) "In counseling and other helping professions, creativity, when combined with the arts frequently results in (a) the production of a tangible product that gives a client insight, such as a piece of writing or a painting, or (b) a process that the clinician formulates, such as a new way of conducting counseling that leads to client change" (p.3).

Research has shown that using creative techniques help students engage, remember content, and more effectively process their thoughts and feelings (Roaten, 2010; Schimmel, 2006/2007, & Walaski, 2009). Counselors are often seeking new ways to engage and/or motivate students who appear to lack investment in counseling. Using talk therapy along with a creative technique can help draw students into the process. Instead of just talking about the issue the creative outlet may offer the student a chance to show a visual picture of the issue or become engaged in the actual process. Just having the materials in the room often generate curiosity and questions.

In addition to student engagement, another benefit of incorporating creative techniques is students are more likely to remember or think about what took place. According to Schimmel (2006-2007), students are more likely to remember content when a visual prop has been used in counseling. Allowing students the opportunity to actually create visual props increases the chance that students remember what took place when "creating" the creation. The creation can be taken with students back to the classroom and/or home; thus increasing the chance of skill transference and further processing.

Lastly, creative techniques can help trigger more accurate expression of inner thoughts and feelings (Waliski, 2009). For example: a counselor may be working with a student who has problems giving into peer pressure. Intellectually and verbally, the student can give reasons he/she should not do certain things and list alternatives to giving in. However, he/she continues to engage in the behavior. Adding a creative technique such as asking the student to create a visual picture (painting, clay art, sand tray depiction, etc) of the battle within may be more appealing and offer more insight into deeper thoughts and feelings.

Counselors continually seek ways to help students process thoughts and feelings and ultimately make choices that empower them to live the life they desire. By coupling a little creativity along with talk therapy, counselors increase the chance of students' lives being changed for the better!

Seek to make a difference as you help students live a meaningful life!

How to Use this Book

There are numerous possibilities of incorporating creative techniques and experiences into counseling! This book is designed to be a jump-start guide for helping professionals to use when working with students individually, in groups, or in the classroom. Sessions are categorized according to topic and are designed to last approximately 30-45 minutes. Of course, some sessions may extend to multiple sessions depending on the creative technique chosen. The following are tips to help you maximize the effectiveness of leading the activities included in this book.

- The term student is a generic term used consistently throughout this text to refer to the client, consumer, person you are working with.
- In most circumstances, the language of the book uses "students." However, almost all sessions can be adapted to use with individuals, small groups, or with classrooms.
- Have all needed materials gathered and ready to use before starting the session.
- Some techniques may be a little messy. Have paper towels and/or cleaning supplies nearby.
- If paint supplies are going to be used, remember to discuss this with the student and/or have an oversized shirt or apron to cover clothing.
- As students enter the environment and ask questions about the materials, use this as an opportunity to let the anticipation build. For example, a student may ask, "What is this stuff for?" You might respond, "We are going to be a little creative today. You will see in a few minutes." Or "What do you predict we are going to do today?"
- Allow students to express themselves with the creation. Avoid the tendency to "tell" or direct the student how to shape things or what color to color things. Allow as much freedom of expression as possible. For example, if you ask them to create a person with dough and they only put one eye on the person, avoid prompting them to add another eye!
- Prompt the student during various times of the creation process to let you in on their world. For example, "Tell me about what you have made so far." "What does this...represent for you?" If the student expresses significant thoughts and/or feelings be sure to allow ample time for him or her to explore these more in depth.
- Please do not feel limited to the discussion questions or topics listed in this book. Explore, explore, explore! Sometimes, when creative expression begins, multiple topics can be addressed. For example, in The Blob session I discussed in the About This Book section, I intended on the session primarily focusing on students processing their thoughts and situations and allowing them to explore ways to make life a little less messy. However, once they engaged in the activity, the room was filled with students working together, giving appropriate feedback to each other, and building friendships! All of those were just by products but excellent session material! Take advantage of those opportunities!
- Even though creative techniques are engaging and fun for many students, they are not for everyone. Please consider the individuality of each student and assess whether an activity is appropriate.
- Adapt the project to your resources and needs. For example, if paint is suggested, you may want to substitute markers. Or instead of making slime, you may want to provide slime that was purchased or pre-made in an effort to reduce the amount of time of the session.
- Sometimes, the counselor may choose to participate in the creative process as well. Feel free to participate but remember to have a purpose (such as to provide a model for a student who is unsure about what to do, to decrease the pressure for a student of someone "watching" them, etc). Avoid making the session about you and your creation!

Bullying & Relational Issues

Dealing with others can be a difficult area of life to navigate. This section helps you lead students to have meaningful discussion and insight into relational dynamics. Issues addressed include bullying, gossiping, friendship, assertiveness, relationship traits, and effective communication/conflict resolution.

Lesson 1: Standing Tall

Overview

Students will gain understanding of decisions and actions that are necessary to combat bullying as they create a character using card stock or paper.

Objectives

- Students will identify and define character traits and/or behaviors that are necessary to combat bullying behavior.
- Students will process and define the traits or behaviors that are most difficult for them to possess or exhibit.
- Students will define action steps for practicing new behaviors and challenging traits within themselves.
- Students will create a person who will serve as a visual reminder of the traits and/or behaviors necessary to combat bullying.

Materials

- Cardstock or any type of paper
- Tape, glue, or stapler
- Scissors
- Pen, pencil, colored pencils, crayons, or marker

Procedures

1. Engage students in a discussion about standing up to bullies. Have them discuss what the person might "look" like, character traits they may possess, and behaviors they may engage in.
2. Have all of the materials listed above out for use. Instruct students to create a person. They can use the materials to create body parts and then staple/tape/glue the parts together. Or they can create a person on one sheet and cut it out. Encourage individual creativity if working with more than one student. It is fine if some students make a small person and others make a large person.

3. Bring up some of the traits and behaviors that were discussed earlier that students felt were necessary to combat bullying. As each trait/behavior is discussed, instruct students to write the word or draw a picture of the behavior onto the person they created. For example, students may agree that courage is necessary. As courage is defined and discussed in depth, students will write the word or draw a picture illustrating courage onto the person they created.

4. Instruct students to create something for the person to have in his/her hand. On the item created (examples–flowers, sword, book), write or draw action steps that the student plans to take to combat bullying.

5. Allow students to take the people home with them to serve as visual reminders of the things discussed. (Other ideas would be to display in classrooms or hallways if done during classroom guidance).

Discussion Questions and Prompts

1. What traits or behaviors are the most difficult for you?

   _____

2. How can you strengthen those weaknesses?

   _____

3. How important is the physical size of a person standing up to a bully?

   _____

4. If you experience or observe bullying what should you do?

   _____

5. Many times students will immediately say, "I will tell a teacher" when asked what to do about bullying. However, studies show that students often do not tell teachers about the incidents. Why is this and what can be done to ensure more bullying is reported? Which traits and behaviors did we talk about today that will need to be strengthened in order for this to occur?

   _____

6. Describe what you will do the next time you experience or witness bullying.

   _____

Lesson 2: Branching Out

Overview

Students will create a tree branch that serves as a visual reminder of the positive attributes of making and having friends.

Objectives

- Students will verbally identify the positive attributes of making and having friends.
- Students will process the attributes of their current friends.
- Students will process the attributes they possess and/or bring to relationships.
- Students will discuss and explore how everyone has different attributes.
- Students will create a tree branch that serves as a visual reminder of the positive attributes of making and having friends.

Materials

- Stick(s)
- String or pipe cleaners
- Paper
- Something to write with
- ** Optional: If you desire to make a full tree (see procedure #2a), you will need a plant pot, some rocks, and several sticks.

Procedures

1. Begin a discussion about friendship. Highlight conversation that specifically identifies positive characteristics of friends or having/making friends.
2. Allow students to create a tree using the materials listed above. If using one stick—allow them to create branches using pipe cleaners or string.
    a.) **If you want to make a full tree—fill the pot with rocks. Place several different sizes of sticks into the rocks.
3. Make leaves from the paper. On the leaves, have students write down the positive attributes that were/are discussed.
4. Attach the leaves to the stick(s) using pipe cleaner or string.

Discussion Questions and Prompts

1. How do you know someone is your friend? What do they do or say?
   How do you know when someone isn't your friend? What do they do or say?

   _____

   _____

2. Describe the positive traits you possess as a friend.

   _____

   _____

3. Describe the positive traits that your friends possess.

   _____

   _____

4. Describe how your tree is like your friendships.

   _____

   _____

Lesson 3: Oops...I Didn't Mean for THAT to Happen

Overview

Students will complete tasks that demonstrate how gossiping can have unintended consequences. Exploration of individual motivation for gossiping will be explored.

Objectives

- Students will discuss and understand the effects of gossip and spreading rumors.
- Students will see a visual example of how spreading gossip and rumors can have unintended consequences.
- Students will see a visual example of how some effects of gossiping and/or spreading rumors are long-term and do not have an easy fix.

Materials

- Small cup or bowl with glitter in it
- A small object to put inside the cup/bowl of glitter (bead, paper clip, tack—just something small)
- Paper
- Copy of **Mouth Motivators** activity sheet for each student
- Tube of toothpaste—any size will work

Procedures

1. Place the small object from the materials list into the cup/bowl with the glitter. Instruct the student(s) to get the object out. Ask them to look at their hands and see what has happened. (At this point, glitter will be on their hands).
2. Ask the students with the glitter on their hands to touch or pick up something else. Discuss what happens.

3. Continue the discussion and make parallels to illustrate how choosing to participate in gossiping/rumor spreading is similar. *Example: Sometimes, we intend on telling one person—and we all know how it goes—it just keeps spreading. Before you know it, it is all over the school or has gotten lots of shares and likes on the internet. The news went much further than you ever intended.*

4. Give the group or student(s) a piece of paper and the tube of toothpaste. Tell them to push the toothpaste out onto the paper.

5. Instruct the students to put the toothpaste back like it was before they started. This is impossible—just like it is impossible to take back some of the destructive effects that gossip/rumors can have on people.

6. Complete the **Mouth Motivators** activity sheet. If done in a group or classroom, please ensure everyone has privacy to encourage honesty.

7. If appropriate for the setting, have a discussion about what came to students' minds as they completed the activity sheets.

Discussion Questions and Prompts

1. What do you gain from gossiping or spreading rumors?

_____

2. Describe how it feels to be the target of gossip or rumor spreading?

_____

3. In today's tech world of internet, social sites, and cell phones—gossip and rumors can spread much faster. What are some long term effects of spreading things electronically? (Make points about future job situations and employers looking at past social media sites, accidentally sending things to the wrong person, etc. If you are working with students and feel it is appropriate, discuss some of the situations in the news media in which students have committed suicide as a result).

_____

_____

Mouth Motivators

Who are you around when you are most likely to gossip?

_____

What feelings do you have while you are gossiping?

_____

What will it take for you to begin making a choice not to participate in gossip?

_____

_____

What action steps can you take to ensure you do not get involved in gossip?

_____

_____

Lesson 4: Clay Wars

Overview

Students will visually process and reconstruct their perceptions of bullies as they learn assertive skills.

Objectives

- Students will create a social narrative using characters created from dough.
- Students will discuss their idea of what a bully is and how one acts.
- Students will rehearse assertiveness skills with counselor feedback and direction.

Materials

- Copy of **Which Ones Work?** handout for each student
- Dough

DOUGH RECIPE

4 cups all purpose flour
1 to 1 ½ cups water

1 cup salt
Optional: food coloring

Combine the flour and salt and mix well. Add approx. ¾ cup of the water and food coloring of your choice to the flour/salt mixture. Add additional water and food coloring as needed until a firm dough, suitable for rolling or patting, is formed.

Additional Notes:

1. This recipe will make 15-20 3□ x 3□ objects. The recipe can be quartered, halved or doubled, etc. depending on your need.

2. If you would like to make one recipe of dough but create different colors, after making the dough, separate it out and then knead the food coloring into the dough. (You may consider wearing rubber gloves if you choose to color the dough this way.)

3. The dough can be stored in air-tight containers or sealed in bags for weeks.

4. If you want the dough to harden—it can be left in open air. If objects are made from the dough—it may take up to 1 week for complete hardening to occur (depending on the amount of humidity in the air). If you would like to expedite the hardening process after objects are made, place the dough in the oven at 300□ for up to 1 hour or until browning begins to occur.

5. You may always substitute with store-bought dough such as Play-Doh© or Crayola Model Magic© (If substituting—follow the package instructions for appropriate hardening processes).

Lesson 4: Clay Wars (CONTINUED)

Procedures

1. Set the scene for the students. *Example: "Today, we are going create a story. You get to be the author. In the story, there will be a bully and at least one other person. Take a few minutes and create your characters."*
2. Encourage students to discuss their characters.
3. Have students use the characters to act out bullying scenes.
4. Use the stories as discussion starters. Provide feedback and suggestions for handling each situation.
5. Discuss effective ways of standing up to bullies using the **Which Ones Work?** activity sheet. Allow students to process which strategies work the best in their setting. Allow students to construct a common bullying scene using the characters they created. Have the characters act out effective strategies in dealing with the problem.
6. Have students re-create the social narratives with the dough characters using different strategies on the activity sheet.

Discussion Questions and Prompts

1. Describe the behavior of bullies.

_____

_____

2. What are the best ways to deal with bullies?

_____

_____

3. At our school, are students and staff dealing effectively with bullies?

_____

4. What can our school and you do differently when dealing with bullies?

_____

_____

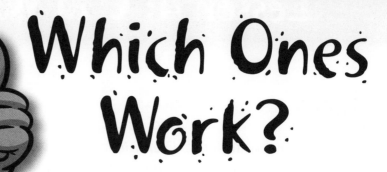

Which Ones Work?

Circle the actions that are most effective in dealing with a bully.

Hitting or Fighting Back

Make a joke about it

Tell a friend

Make plans to get back at them

Do nothing   **Tell an adult at home**

Pretend it doesn't bother you

Walk away   **Tell the person(s) to stop**

Remind yourself it is not your fault

Tell an adult at school

Tell the bully how you feel

Lesson 5: Throwing Stones

Overview

Students will create two pieces of rock art that symbolize the choice to speak words that build others up or tear others down.

Objectives

- Students will process the power of words for building up or destroying.
- Students will discuss the control they must exercise over their words.
- Students will create a piece of art that serves as a visual reminder of choosing words that build instead of destroy.

Materials

- A container of rocks
- Paint or permanent markers
- Hot glue gun (if students want to attach rocks together)

Procedures

1. Begin a discussion about how powerful things are (examples—show pictures of a raging river that is used as a source of power for the area; other examples include muscles, wind, sun, etc.). Discuss the effects of power giving examples of how the power is often good but can be destructive. *Example: The river's power can be used to operate plants that produce clothing or automobiles. That same power can also be used to throw a kayaker into a rock and crush a bone or two!* Lead into discussing the power of the words we choose to speak.
2. Have students process the concept of the power of words using some of the discussion questions and prompts that follow.
3. Discuss how to make the choice to use words that build. Students may want to write reminders of the points that are made during this part of the discussion onto the rocks they will use to make their piece of art.
4. Allow students to create a piece of art using the rocks that will serve as a visual reminder for them to choose words that build instead of destroy (examples—paint rocks and write positive words on them; build a tower with the rocks with words that "build" on each rock; paint or draw "build" on one rock and "destroy" on the other).

Lesson 5: Throwing Stones (CONTINUED)

Discussion Questions and Prompts

1. How can words be powerful?

   _____

   _____

2. Share some words that have been spoken to you that helped build you up.
   Share some words that have been spoken to you that have been destructive.

   _____

   _____

3. How does a person decide what words to use?

   _____

4. When are you tempted to use words that are destructive?

   _____

5. What is gained from using destructive words? What is lost by using destructive words?

   _____

   _____

6. What is gained from using words that build? What is lost by using words that build?

   _____

   _____

Lesson 6: A REAL FRIEND?

Overview

Students will create a plaque with desirable friendship qualities inscribed on it to serve as a reminder of how to be a good friend and how to determine who true friends really are.

Objectives

- Students will identify qualities of true friendship.
- Students will evaluate their roles in friendships in comparison to the qualities they list.
- Students will design and create a plaque that reminds them of the desirable qualities of a friend.

Materials

- Toothpicks (one for each student)
- Wax or parchment paper for rolling and drying
- Dough recipe (page 16)
- ** *Optional: You can go ahead and roll/cut the dough into plaques and dry them. Then, students can use markers or paint to write on them.*

Procedures

1. Encourage students to describe the perfect friendship. Highlight desirable qualities as students discuss them. Make sure to point out that even in great friendships, conflicts and misunderstandings still occur. However, even in times of conflict there can be desirable ways to handle conflict in friendships—have students discuss these as well.
2. Allow students to mold the dough into a plaque (no rules on the creation—they get to decide).
3. Use the toothpick to inscribe the qualities of friendship they think are important into the plaque. Encourage them to add any type of decorative element to the design. Plaques will need to dry—refer to the recipe for drying instructions.
4. If you already had the plaques made prior to the session, allow students to use paint or markers to design their plaques.

Lesson 6: A REAL FRIEND? (CONTINUED)

Discussion Questions and Prompts

1. Describe the qualities of a perfect friend.

   _____

   _____

2. All friendships generally have some type of conflict at some point—how can conflict be handled in positive ways?

   _____

   _____

3. How do you measure up in comparison to the desirable quality list?

   _____

   _____

4. What are some areas you need to improve on?

   _____

   _____

5. What happens when you see that some of your friends continually exhibit undesirable friendship qualities? How can you handle this in a way that would model positive qualities?

   _____

   _____

Lesson 7: Rock Solid

Overview

While processing characteristics that may indicate if someone is trustworthy/dependable or not, students will design a large rock with representations of things that are dependable and trustworthy in their lives.

Objectives

- Students will identify people, places, and themes that are dependable and trustworthy in their lives.
- Students will identify indicators/redflags that suggest a person may not be trustworthy/dependable.
- Students will design and create a large rock with representations of the things that are dependable in their lives.

Materials

- 1 Large rock or stone (these can usually be obtained by contacting the state highway department office, a local stone company, or from a local river)
- ** *Optional: If a large rock/stone cannot be located, use the handout,* **Rock Steady.**
- Any type of materials students may want to use to decorate the rock (jewels, paper, cardstock, beads, sequins, paint, markers, etc.)
- Hot glue gun—if students are going to attach things to the rock

Procedures

1. Discuss and define the concepts of dependability and trustworthiness. Specifically have students discuss the "evidence" that makes one dependable or trustworthy. Encourage student(s) to give specific examples of times people have shown themselves to be trustworthy/dependable or when they have not.
2. To demonstrate the concept, stand on a stable chair, stool, step ladder, etc. Explain how you are choosing to stand on the object because you trust it is going to hold you up. Next, lean forward a small amount and explain that while you trust the object to hold you up at some point if you keep leaning forward you must trust more fully or realize the chair is no longer going to be dependable/trustworthy to support you. Lead into a discussion about how oftentimes in relationships with people (especially bullies) we have to assess whether we need to continue to trust more fully or to make a determination that a person/circumstance is not going to be the best for us.

3. Discuss common indicators in relationships with others that suggest the person/circumstance may not be trustworthy/dependable. Take this opportunity to discuss relationships in which one is bullied and/or taken advantage of by others.

4. Have students identify things, relationships, people, themes, etc. that have been dependable/trustworthy during their lives. Let them creatively represent the items by making a list, designing symbols/objects to attach to the large rock, or by writing/drawing directly onto the rock. Give students time to decorate the rock however they choose.

5. While students are working on their creation, take the opportunity to discuss what to do when one finds themselves in a relationship in which someone is not dependable and/or trustworthy.

Discussion Questions and Prompts

1. Tell about an experience in which a person was trustworthy and/or dependable.

   _____

2. What evidence (action in a person's life) indicates if a person is trustworthy and/or dependable?

   _____

3. What are the results when a person is not trustworthy or dependable?

   _____

4. What are some indicators ("red flags") that suggest a person may not be trustworthy and/or dependable?

   _____

5. Oftentimes, in relationships people cannot see the "red flags" that indicate a person is not trustworthy/dependable. What do you think blinds people to these signs?

   _____

6. Rate yourself on a scale of 1-5 on a dependable/trustworthiness scale. Give specific examples of why you chose the rating you did.

   _____

7. What should you do when you find yourself in a relationship in which someone is not trustworthy and/or dependable?

   _____

Rock Steady

Directions: Identify things, relationships, people, themes, etc. that have been dependable/trustworthy during your life. Creatively represent the items by writing or designing symbols/objects to attach to the rock.

_____   _____

_____   _____

_____   _____

Lesson 8: My Way, Your Way, Our Way

Overview

Students will practice effective communication/conflict resolution skills while creating a collage together.

Objectives

- Students will discuss and demonstrate effective communication strategies.
- Students will discuss and demonstrate effective conflict resolution skills.
- Students will work with other students to create a group collage project.

Materials

- Any type of material in which pictures can be cut from or created (magazines, paper/pencil for drawing, cards, old books, etc.)
- A piece of paper, bulletin board paper or poster board for the collage to be made upon
- Markers/colored pencils, etc., if students are going to create their own pictures
- Glue sticks/glue

Procedures

1. Lead a discussion about how it feels to work with a group. Point out times when it can be frustrating and rewarding. Allow the group to process different scenarios. Make them relevant to your student as you highlight the feelings that would be evoked within the situations. For example: What if someone was exhibiting bullying behavior in the group? What if the group never liked your ideas? What if you never liked any of the group ideas and thought yours were better?

2. After a few minutes of processing the scenarios, discuss how one can communicate with the group effectively when he or she may feel frustrated. To facilitate students "experiencing" effective and non-effective ways to communicate, with a very loud, threatening/rude voice tone say, "It is not always about what you say, but how you say it." Repeat the sentence using a calm tone. Allow time for discussion. Some simple rules of effective communication can be presented.

   1. Talk using a calm voice.
   2. Clearly communicate what you would like and/or feel using "I" statements.
   3. Ask for feedback regarding what you communicated.

3. Discuss what happens when you have made an effort to communicate effectively but conflict still occurs. Review conflict resolution skills that have previously been taught or use the following.

   1. Take time to cool down if you are having an intense feeling.
   2. Using effective communication skills, clearly communicate your desire.
   3. Listen to the other party(ies).
   4. Give feedback.
   5. Work to resolution by seeking compromise.

   Discuss compromise and have students give specific examples.

4. Explain that the students are going to create a group collage of pictures. Encourage them to use effective communication skills to resolve any conflicts that may arise. If the students are older, allow them to decide on a theme for the collage and continue. For younger students, you may want to assign them a theme, such as: things _____ graders love, happiness is…, nature, effective communication & conflict resolution, etc. If your students are unfamiliar with a collage, explain that it is a collection of pictures that represent a given idea. Expound/discuss as needed.

5. While students are working on the collage, point out when effective communication and conflict resolution skills are used.

Lesson 8: My Way, Your Way, Our Way (CONTINUED)

Discussion Questions and Prompts

1. What can be frustrating when working in groups or with other people?

_____

2. What can be rewarding when working in groups or other people?

_____

3. If you are working in a group and someone is exhibiting bullying behavior, what should you do?

_____

4. What are some things you should remember when trying to communicate with others more effectively?

_____

5. What if you have communicated what you want and the group or the other person doesn't agree?

_____

6. What are some successful conflict resolution strategies?

_____

7. What is compromise? How can compromise be achieved?

_____

Lesson 9: It Sticks With You

Overview

Students will explore properties of materials as connections are made about relationships and dealing with difficult people.

Objectives

- Students will explore and identify the properties of materials.
- Students will use comparisons to describe the properties of materials and relationships.
- Students will understand the effects of actions and choices in relationships.

Materials

Please feel free to pick/choose which substances/objects you use. It is not necessary to have them all.
- A sticky substance/object (examples: glue, honey, jelly, sticky hands)
- A wet substance (examples: water or any other liquid)
- A hard object (examples: rocks, marbles, beads)
- Soft objects (examples: cotton balls, play dough or dough made from recipe in this book, toilet paper, craft balls/pompom balls)
- Sound objects (examples: maracas, bells-hand or small holiday jingle bells, container of paper clips, baby rattle)
- Something to put each object in (examples: bags, cups, bowls)
- A bowl of water/hand towel for washing/drying hands
- ** *Optional: blindfold*
- ** *Optional: Copy of handout, **Exploring Situations** (if needed)*

Procedures

1. Begin a discussion about relationships and dealing with other people. Explain that for the most part, we generally like ourselves, our ideas, and our attitudes. However, when we have to interact with others, we encounter different ideas, attitudes and different ways of relating. Ask students to share experiences they have had as they interact with others. Discuss how we can easily interact with some people while on the other hand, we find it difficult to interact with others. Make sure to allow students an opportunity to share and make connections with the others or yourself.

2. Explain that you have several objects and/or substances that are going to be explored. Ask students to describe the properties of each item. Encourage them to come up with comparisons of relationships/dealing with other people by using the properties of the substances/objects.

3. Allow students to touch/explore the objects. If you want, blindfold students as they explore the objects or have the objects covered with a blindfold and allow students to put their hands under the covering to explore.

4. As each object is explored, discuss how the properties compare to relating to people. In case you need some help facilitating the comparisons, refer to the handout, **Exploring Situations**. Please remember the more involved students become, the more meaningful the experience will be for them. Allow them to discuss how to handle the situations they share.

5. Have students pick which properties are most like them in personality and interaction styles. Encourage them to explain why and have a discussion about how these characteristics/properties affect their relationships/dealings with others.

Discussion Questions and Prompts

1. Why do you think it is easy to get along with some people and difficult to get along with others?

_____

2. Share some experiences you have had trying to interact with others (positive and negative experiences).

_____

3. Have you ever found yourself in a sticky situation in which you were tempted to do something you really did not want to do? What did you do? Are you ever around someone who has some negative attitudes, etc. and after being around them for a while you find yourself doing the same things?

_____

4. When you hear the term "hard people" what comes to your mind? Tell experiences you have had with people who are hard. What do you think makes a person come across as hard? What life experiences do you think they have had that contribute to the way they interact with others?

_____

5. What impact do you have on others? How have others impacted you? What is a positive experience with a person that has impacted you? What is a negative experience with a person that has impacted you?

_____

Exploring Situations

STICKY SUBSTANCES

- *Bullying:* Oftentimes you run across someone and realize you are in a sticky situation. Myabe you are dealing with a bully. On one hand, you want the behavior to stop but on the other hand, you are afraid to do anything because you think it will get worse. This can be a really sticky situation.

- *Bullying/Gossip/Words:* Things others say to you (or that you say to others) have a tendency to stick with you.

- *Peer pressure:* Sometimes when you are around others, the things they do have a tendency to stick to you—like negative attitudes and pressure to do things you are uncomfortable doing.

WET SUBSTANCES

- *Bullying/difficult people:* Feeling wet is oftentimes irritating and uncomfortable. Have you ever gotten your socks wet and tried walking in your shoes? How was that? When dealing with difficult people/ bullies, you can be overcome with lots of uncomfortable emotions: anger, guilt, frustration, hopelessness, fear. On the flip side, being wet can also be refreshing. Have you ever jumped in a cool pool on a hot day? Standing up to bullies/difficult people can be rewarding and great learning experiences.

- *All aspects of relationships—positive and negative:* After touching a wet substance, your hands are left with an impact. The people you interact with, whether positive or negative leave an impact on your life. You leave an impact on others' lives as well.

HARD OBJECTS

- *Bullying/Dealing with difficult people:* Sometimes people who experience lots of hurt, rejection, disappointments, and other negative emotions become hardened people. They come across as very tough and/or unapproachable on the exterior.

- *Gossiping/Relational actions:* Hard things can be destructive and break things. Throw a rock into some glass and see what happens.

Exploring Situations

Our words and actions, when hard, can destroy relationships and leave people with wounds. Hard things are also good for building things up/making them stronger. Our words and actions can be used for the same!

- *Kind words/Encouragement:* Oftentimes, we feel weighed down with life…hardened. Someone's words and/or actions can sometimes help us carry the burden or make the load lighter.

SOFT OBJECTS

- *Bullying/Assertiveness:* These objects can be squeezed and shaped into what we want. Oftentimes, when we are dealing with bullies/difficult people we just go along and do whatever they want instead of standing up for ourselves.

- *Relational actions:* Soft things can often be comforting. I prefer a soft place to lay down. How about you? Sometimes when we are hurting, a comforting word or kind gesture can bring hope and healing.

- *Dealing with relational issues:* Soft things are often absorbent. Sometimes, we can take a lot in life and keep going. Other times, when dealing with too much, we can get over-saturated and need help from others.

SOUND OBJECTS

- *Bullying/Difficult people:* People who often make the most noise are the ones who follow through with the least action.

- *Bullying/Assertiveness:* Have you ever heard the saying, 'the squeaky wheel gets the oil?' Sometimes, speaking/standing up for yourself sets a boundary for others and clearly communicates that you will not allow an unacceptable behavior/action to continue. A bully may quickly realize that he/she has picked the wrong target.

- *Bullying/Gossiping:* Too much noise can be irritating. Running your mouth all the time with vain words, untruths, and downgrading words can really damage relationships. People generally want to get away from things that are irritating.

Lesson 10: Words with Others

Overview

Students will create word rocks to exchange or give to others that symbolize words that define their relationships (or that they would like to define the relationship).

Objectives

- Students will identify traits of positive relationships.
- Students will identify traits of negative relationships.
- Students will identify positive relationships they have with people.
- Students will identify defining words for their present relationships.

Materials

- Rocks/gravel (just large enough for words to be written on)
- Markers and/or paint for designing rocks
- Newspaper or scrap paper (to place the rocks on while designing and drying)
- Copy of handout, **Relationship Chart** for each student

Procedures

1. Facilitate a discussion about relationships. Discuss the differences in relationships—friends, parents, teachers, people in class with you, etc. Highlight that all relationships have differences, some positive and some negative. Allow students to process some positive and negative traits of relationships.
2. Distribute copies of the **Relationship Chart** to all students. Instruct students to list all the relationships they have with others that they can think of. Ask them to brainstorm a defining word for each relationship. The word can be a trait that describes the relationship or a word they wish described the relationship. Instruct them to write the word on the chart.
3. After words have been created on the chart, distribute rocks to students. Tell them to pick out a relationship and design a rock with the defining word on it. If you have enough materials and time, allow students to make more than one. Encourage students to paint and/or use marker to decorate the rocks. Once the background is decorated, encourage them to write the defining word onto the rock.

Lesson 10: Words with Others (CONTINUED)

4. Once the rocks are finished, discuss how they can use the rocks to help open up discussions within their relationships. They can give the rocks to others and explain the meaning to them. They can ask the people they are in a relationship with to design a rock and they can talk about the expectations each have for the relationship.

Discussion Questions and Prompts

1. What are some traits that characterize negative relationships?

_____

_____

2. What are some traits that characterize positive relationships?

_____

_____

3. Think about a relationship you have with someone (ex: parents, friend, teacher, bully, etc.). What word would you chose to define the relationship?

_____

_____

4. If a relationship is not ideal or positive, what word would you chose to characterize that relationship in its present state? What word would you like to be able to choose for that relationship?

_____

_____

5. How would it be if you choose to give the other person in the relationship the rock with the word you chose? How would they respond?

_____

_____

Relationship Chart

Directions: List the relationships you have with others. List the defining word for the relationship in the other column.

RELATIONSHIP	DEFINING WORD

Lesson 11: Deposits or Withdrawals

Overview

Students will create a bank while discussing the concept of how our words and actions either make a deposit in a relationship or a withdrawal.

Objectives

- Students will process their words and actions in relation to others.
- Students will be able to identify actions and words as deposits or withdrawals.
- Students will create a bank as a visual to serve as a reminder of this concept.

Materials

- Empty plastic bottles (water/soda bottles) with tops
  ** *Optional: You can use envelopes, shoe boxes, or small plastic containers instead of bottles.*
- Art supplies for decorating the bottles (examples: permanent markers, paint, paper, small rocks or pieces of sticks/wood to attach for legs, yarn/string, duct tape)
- Knife for cutting the opening
  ** *Optional: You may consider cutting the openings once students have finished their creations and you are alone, due to safety concerns.*
- Scrap paper/newspaper for placing under the creation, if paint will be used

Procedures

1. Discuss how we relate to others can partially be understood using the concept of a bank. Highlight how at a bank, deposits and withdrawals are made. Make sure students understand both concepts. Discuss how we choose with our actions and words to make deposits or withdrawals in relationships.
2. Allow opportunities for the students to make this concept real. Encourage discussion and share examples of words/actions that have added to a relationship and words/actions that have made a withdrawal from a relationship. If they are reluctant to share or seem unsure of the concept, offer some scenarios that may be common issues for the students. Examples may include:
   - A person in your math class makes it a point every day to offer negative comments about your appearance. ***Deposit or Withdrawal?***

- Your teacher writes a note on your science assignment that points out how well written and thought-out your work is. ***Deposit or Withdrawal?***
- You worked really hard to keep your room clean. Your mom walks in and the first thing she notices is your jacket laying the floor. ***Deposit or Withdrawal?***
- Walking down the hallway, a random person smiles and holds the door open for you. ***Deposit or Withdrawal?***

3. Encourage students to identify people with whom they interact. Allow them to discuss how their interactions are swayed—deposits or withdrawals. *Examples: With your parents, are your words/actions more deposits or withdrawals? With your teachers, are your words more deposits or withdrawals?*

4. While having the discussion above (or after the discussion), allow students to create a bank. Explain that the idea is that the bank will serve as a visual reminder of the concept of deposits or withdrawals. Encourage students each time they see the bank, to make an effort to deposit into a relationship or during an interaction. Examples of some bank design ideas include: stand the bottle up vertically, add paper wings and create a spaceship or rocket; turn it on its side, add some small rocks/sticks for legs and create a 4-legged animal.

Discussion Questions and Prompts

1. What are the purposes of banks? How do you think the concept of a bank can also apply to relationships?

_____

2. How do your actions and words affect others? Tell of a time when someone's actions/words had a positive effect on you. Tell of a time when someone's actions/words had a negative effect on you.

_____

3. What are some actions/words that make deposits with others? What are some actions/words that make withdrawals with others?

_____

4. What happens when you are in a relationship or have to constantly interact with someone who only makes withdrawals?

_____

5. When examining your relationships, what can you do to improve your deposit/withdrawal transaction ratio?

_____

Self-Regulation: Emotional Expression

Students often struggle with impulsivity and inappropriately expressing emotions. These self-regulation activities help lead students to process more effective ways of communicating what they want and how they feel.

Lesson 12: Calm Down

Overview

Students will conduct scientific test trials to determine which is the quickest way to get to the bottom of a cup. The connection will be evident that sometimes the best practice is to pace ourselves and act slowly even though our senses or feelings sometimes tell us to hurry up!

Objectives

- Students will practice how to come up with different strategies when one is unsuccessful.
- Students will be able to visually see and experience that sometimes the best solution is to be patient and not rush to do things.
- Students will be able to process the differences between their feelings/senses and having self-regulation.

Materials

- A penny or small object to place at the bottom of the container
- A bowl of water/hand towel to rinse fingers
- A stop watch or timer
- A copy of **Calm Down Chart** to record trials
- Pencils for recording results
- One batch of **What is this Stuff?** using the recipe below
- ** *Note: Depending on how many students you are working with, you may want to divide the batch into small containers. If you are working with one student or a small group, one container would be sufficient.*

WHAT IS THIS STUFF? RECIPE

2 cups corn starch   1 cup water
bowl   *optional food coloring

Mix the corn starch, water, and food coloring together in a bowl. The mixture will "feel" difficult to stir. Just turn the spoon slowly. Efforts to rush this process will not be successful!

Procedures

1. Just for fun, show students the container(s) of **What is this Stuff?**. Allow them to guess what it is and what it will be used for during the session.

2. Begin a discussion about impulsivity. Use examples that are relevant to your students (not controlling emotions, making decisions without thinking, rushing through work, saying the first thing that comes to your mind, etc.).

3. Explain that you all are going to conduct a scientific experiment to learn about self-regulation and changing strategies. Depending on the knowledge level of the group, you may need to discuss the concept of self-regulation (self-control).

4. Give the student or groups of students a container of **What is this Stuff?** with a penny or small object at the bottom, a copy of the **Calm Down Chart**, and a stopwatch or timer for recording time.

5. Go over the instructions on the chart. Explain the goal of the experiment is to recover the object from the bottom of the container. Have the student(s) identify their strategy—how they plan to retrieve the object and record it on the chart. Once recorded, instruct them to time themselves and see how long it takes to retrieve the item. After the time is recorded, allow the group to make observations about the task, etc. Encourage them to record the observations/notes.

6. Discuss with the students how they plan to change their strategy. Explain how sometimes we just need to stay calm and not rush through things. Just take a slow and steady approach. Point out that sometimes when we have new information or a result we are not proud of, the best course of action is to change what we do (our strategy). Allow student(s) to continue the other two trials following the same method.

7. Use the experiment to make reference to student(s)' lives. Here are a few examples:
   - "Sometimes, we look at things and feel like we know best. So instead of getting all the information or trying to make a more wise decision, we just act. Some of you figured the best way to get to the bottom was to push your fingers down as fast as you could into the substance. What happened when you did that?"
   - "Have you ever felt an emotion that is so strong you just acted on the emotion without thinking? Maybe you just impulsively told someone exactly what you thought about them. As soon as they walked off, you felt terrible. In hindsight, you wished you had given yourself a minute to calm down. Just like in the experiment, we sometimes have to change strategies. When we find ourselves acting impulsively, we need to evaluate the results of our actions. If they are not pleasant, then we need to consider making some changes—which may include using some self-control."

Lesson 12: Calm Down (CONTINUED)

Discussion Questions and Prompts

1. What happened when you tried to force your finger/hands to the bottom of the substance?

   _____

   _____

2. What strategy worked best?

   _____

   _____

3. Tell about a time you made a decision without thinking and the result was not what you wanted.

   _____

   _____

4. Tell about a time you were overwhelmed with an emotion and chose to act on the emotion instead of trying to wait and think more clearly.

   _____

   _____

5. If you act impulsively and do not like the result, does it make sense to act in the same way again? Why or why not?

   _____

   _____

6. What are some self-regulation (self-control) strategies that you can use when you feel the need to act impulsively?

   _____

   _____

Calm Down Chart

Directions: Chart the time it takes to find the object. List the strategy you used during each trial. For example, did you push your fingers as hard as you could or did you just let them fall into the substance? Make any helpful notes and observations you or your team notice.

	Time to Find Object	Strategy	Notes/ Observations
Time Trial # 1			
Time Trial # 2			
Time Trial # 3			

Lesson 13: Bottled Up

Overview

Students will conduct two experiments and make observations of what happens when one keeps feelings/emotions within too long. Appropriate ways to release emotions are introduced.

Objectives

- Students will process emotions that they feel are just waiting to be released.
- Students will discuss what happens when emotions are not expressed adequately.
- Students will identify appropriate ways to express emotions.

Materials

- An empty plastic bottle (water/soda bottle)
- Baking Soda
- Vinegar
- A bowl or sink to catch the overflow from the bottle
- Balloon
- Piece of paper to use as a funnel or a small funnel

Procedures

1. Discuss the challenges of appropriately expressing emotions. Allow students to give examples of times when they have had an outburst of anger, sadness, or overexcitement that did not have the best results. Explain that knowing how and when to express emotions can get complicated. Encourage students to discuss these challenges. For example, sometimes when we are overwhelmed with anger, we allow our words and/or actions to get out of control. This often leads to feelings of regret or damages relationships. Having skills to adequately express the anger would allow us to have some emotional release without suffering from the negative consequences of unrestrained emotional expression.

2. Explain that two experiments will be conducted to highlight what happens with our emotions. For the first, place the bottle in a bowl or sink. Using a funnel, pour 1/4 cup baking soda into the bottle. Discuss how the baking soda represents emotions that are felt but never expressed. Point out that the baking soda just sits there—it does not go away. Allow students to predict what is going to happen when you add another ingredient. Pour 1/2 cup of vinegar into the bottle. Encourage students to describe what happened.

Highlight that the vinegar caused an eruption. Explain that sometimes when we try to keep our emotions bottled up (never expressing them appropriately) we experience a trigger and our emotions explode–leading us to say and do things we regret or that damage relationships. Encourage students to identify what triggers their emotional eruptions.

3. For the second experiment, place 2 tablespoons of baking soda into the balloon using a funnel. (This is easier if you blow up the balloon first and then deflate it prior to putting the baking soda in the balloon.) Inside the bottle (rinse it out from the first experiment), pour 1/2 cup of vinegar. Allow students to predict what will happen when the balloon is placed onto the bottle. After predictions are made, place the balloon around the opening of the bottle. Tilt the balloon upright so the baking soda will fall into the vinegar. As the reaction occurs, the balloon should inflate from the pressure. Discuss with the students that when the baking soda/vinegar react, carbon dioxide is created. The gas creates pressure inside the bottle and must escape, therefore it inflates the balloon. Explain that when we experience strong emotion, it is important to release some of the pressure that builds within.

4. Encourage students to discuss appropriate ways to express emotion. Some suggestions, in case the students need prompting, include: art (drawing/painting,etc.), writing, physical activity (dance, exercise), allowing yourself a cool-down time before expressing feelings verbally, deep breathing, and positive self-talk. As students discuss suggestions, ask them to give specific examples of how each suggestion would help.

Discussion Questions and Prompts

1. Explain what happens when you feel a strong emotion but never express it–you just keep it inside.

_____

2. Tell about a time you allowed an emotion to keep building up inside.

_____

3. If you never express or deal with your emotions, do they just go away?

_____

4. Have you ever experienced several emotions at one time? Explain.

_____

5. What are some ways that you can adequately express your emotions?

_____

Lesson 14: The Blob

Overview

Students learn to process how one can make positive choices even when one's circumstance can feel/look very messy.

Objectives

- Students will verbally describe their current "situation."
- Students will identify areas of their current situation that are frustrating or feel out of control.
- Students will identify areas in their lives in which they have a sense of control.
- Students will begin to process positive choices they can make despite their messy circumstance.

Materials

- Slime
** *Optional: Zip-top bags for each student (if they are taking the slime home)*

SLIME RECIPE

4 oz White Glue (washable glues do not work as well)
1 1/2 cup of water
2 containers—bowls or cups

1 tsp Borax (found in store's laundry aisle)
Food coloring (optional)
2 stirring spoons

In one container, stir together 4 oz. of white glue with ½ cup water. *Optional—add food coloring to the mixture; otherwise, it will be white.

In a separate container, mix 1 cup of water with 1 teaspoon of borax.

Slowly, stir the glue recipe into the borax mixture.

Pick up the slime that forms and knead with your hands until it feels dry. Discard the remaining water.

The more the slime is played with, the less sticky and firmer it will become.

Recipe copied from http://chemistry.about.com/cs/howtos/ht/slime.htm

---

Lesson 14: The Blob (CONTINUED)

Procedures

1. Introduce the topic to be discussed. *Example: "Today we are going to look at areas in our lives that feel messy or out of control. Sometimes this just means that we do not like what is happening or we wish we could change something. Other times, when we are faced with these messy things, we lose control. We may yell, scream, fight, or cry. Today, as we look at these areas in our lives, we are going to create a mess. Let's get started."*

2. Lead a discussion about these "messy" areas of our lives. Help students identify and process things they feel, ways they react, and how they wish the situations were different.

3. Lead the discussion to the slime creation. *Example: "I told you earlier we were going to create a mess. Here we go."* Guide students through the slime recipe to create the slime.

4. Discuss the properties of the slime (how it feels, what it does when it touches something or when it is laid on an item, etc.).

5. Engage the student(s) with the discussion questions listed below.

** *Optional: Allow the student to take the slime home by packaging it in a zip-top bag. In order for the slime to remain intact, it should be stored in a refrigerator.*

Discussion Questions and Prompts

1. How is the slime like the messy situation in your life?

_____

2. What are some of the areas in your situation that you can control?

_____

3. How does it feel when you find yourself being faced with the messy situation?

_____

4. When you find yourself in the messy situation, what are some choices that you can make that are positive?

_____

5. Do you ever "lose control" of your feelings or actions and make a situation even more messy? Tell me about a time that has happened.

_____

6. Tell about a time your choices have helped make a situation "less messy."

_____

Lesson 15: A Visual Memory

Overview

Students will create a 3-D scene depicting memories of a loved one, pet, or situation in which loss has occurred.

Objectives

- Students will identify times they have dealt with a loss.
- Students will process the emotions associated with a loss.
- Students will create scenes of memories to depict times of loss.

Materials

- Wax or butcher paper for molding/drying (or just a flat table/desktop)
- Dough recipe (page 16)

Procedures

1. Give students a portion of the dough.
2. Discuss the concept of a loss. Point out that death is not the only time in which people experience loss. Examples of other losses include: loss of relationship due to break-up, move, divorce, etc.; loss of peace due to struggles in life. Encourage students to share their losses.
3. Encourage students to share positive memories of the thing(s) they lost. Lead a discussion that it is ok to celebrate the positive memories of the special situations, relationships, etc. Explain how sometimes when we experience loss, we have such strong emotions of anger, sadness, etc. that we forget it is ok to remember the good things/times.
4. Instruct students that they will use the dough to create a scene that represents positive memories for them. For example, if the person has lost a relationship he/she may want to create things/symbols with the dough that represent things they liked about the relationship (i.e., a heart might represent love, a small hand may represent help, a smiley face may represent laughing).

Lesson 15: A Visual Memory *(CONTINUED)*

Discussion Questions and Prompts

1. When we say someone has experienced a loss, what are we saying?

2. Share about a loss you have experienced. What emotions did/do you experience?

3. What are some effective ways you have dealt with your loss?

4. When thinking about the memories associated with the person, relationship, situation or thing, what emotions do you feel?

Lesson 16: Feelings Museum

Overview

Students will create a feelings display using rocks to assist in identifying and expressing feelings.

Objectives

- Students will expand their feeling vocabulary.
- Students will be able to understand the concept of feeling intensity.
- Students will identify their feelings using symbols.

Materials

- Rocks
- Paint or permanent markers
- ** *Optional: any embellishments for decorating the rocks you chose to make available*
- Copy of **Feeling Vocabulary** for each student

Procedures

1. Begin with a discussion about feelings. Have students identify as many feelings as possible. Explore with students how they decide which words to use when describing their feelings. For example: If you are afraid, how do you decide to say, "I was nervous" versus "I was terrified"? Discuss the concept of feeling intensity. Sometimes we feel things very strongly and other times we have the same feeling but at a lower level. If the students have a hard time understanding the concept, use a thermometer as an example.
2. Distribute copies of **Feeling Vocabulary** to each student. Allow them time to read over the lists. Ask them to identify words they have never heard or do not understand. Discuss the words with the students and have them share scenarios in which a particular word would be chosen over another.
3. Lead students to identify the feelings they have felt so far during the day. Instruct them to choose a rock for each feeling. Explain that for each feeling, they will decorate a rock that demonstrates (or puts on display) the feeling. Ask them to pretend the rock(s) are going to be a part of a museum display for that word.

Lesson 16: Feelings Museum (CONTINUED)

Discussion Questions and Prompts

1. Name as many feelings as you can.

   _____

   _____

2. When you express your feelings to others, how do you choose which word to use? For example: When would you say I am terrified versus I was a little nervous?

   _____

   _____

3. What does intensity mean? What are some words that would indicate that I was mildly happy? Extremely happy? A little mad? Extremely mad?

   _____

   _____

4. If (insert feeling word) were put on display in a museum, what would it look like?

   _____

   _____

Feelings Vocabulary

HAPPY

overjoyed, thrilled, ecstatic, delighted, relieved, satisfied, content, glad, fine, pleased, cheerful, great, lucky, fortunate, merry, festive, jubilant, playful, calm, peaceful, energetic, gleeful, bright, blessed, beaming, chirpy, upbeat, elated, radiant

SAD

unhappy, dissatisfied, blue, upset, down, heartbroken, sorrowful, hurt, left out, depressed, disappointed, alone, hopeless, regretful, sorrowful, desperate, grieved, mournful, dismayed, suspicious, alarmed, inferior, ashamed, guilty, embarrassed, miserable, sulky

MAD/ANGRY

irritated, annoyed, agitated, perturbed, uptight, hot, disgusted, irate, outraged, furious, touchy, hostile, bitter, provoked, inflamed, cross, boiling, fuming, shaky, restless, cowardly, resentful

AFRAID

anxious, nervous, unsure, timid, terrified, petrified, scared, frightened, insecure, uneasy, shocked, panicky, apprehensive, worried, fearful, horrified, uncertain, hesitant, distressed, rattled

Lesson 17: Oh Yeah...I Almost Forgot

Overview

Create a symbol that serves as a reminder that one can make positive choices when angry or experiencing other overwhelming emotions.

Objectives

- Discuss the concept of logos and symbols.
- Process objects, things, symbols that have meaning for the students.
- Students will identify one emotion they frequently experience that is overwhelming.
- Create a symbol that can serve as a reminder that positive choices can be made even when one is experiencing overwhelming emotions.
- Plan where the symbol will be placed so that it will help offer support for the student outside of the counseling setting.
- If appropriate/needed, outline an action plan associated with the symbol. This may include allowing the object to serve as a prompt to begin an action plan (example: begin a relaxation technique, ask for help or a timeout, etc.).

Materials

- Dough recipe (page 16)
- Straw or toothpick (only if making a hole in the object to hang)
- Wax paper or other surface appropriate for drying
- ** *Optional: rolling pin or glass for rolling dough*
- ** *Optional: cookie sheet (If you would like to expedite the drying process, you can warm the object in the oven at 300° for up to 1 hour or until the objects begin browning.)*
- ** *Optional: decorative embellishments (glitter, gems, sequins, toothpicks for engraving, ribbon, feathers, etc.)*
- Copy of **What Does This Mean**? handout

Lesson 17: Oh Yeah...I Almost Forgot

(CONTINUED)

Procedures

1. Prepare dough prior to the session or allow the student(s) to prepare the dough.
2. Introduce the activity by discussing and/or showing pictures of symbols/logos from the **What Does This Mean?** worksheet. Discuss the concept behind the symbol. For example: What does the picture of the man/woman prompt us to do? What does it mean to us? Highlight the fact that the symbols remind us/prompt us to know or do something. Explain that each student is going to create a symbol that will serve as a prompt or reminder that positive choices can be made even when one is experiencing overwhelming emotions.
3. Allow students to process/discuss things, objects, and colors that are meaningful to them. Let them explain what each thing means or represents to them.
4. Allow students adequate time to create his/her own symbol.
5. Symbols can be left in the room for drying (will take about 1 week) or can be dried in the oven as directed in the materials section.

Discussion Questions and Prompts

1. What are the purposes of symbols?

   _____

2. What feeling do you experience that is hard for you to deal with?

   _____

3. What things can serve as a reminder to you when you feel _____ to make positive choices?

   _____

4. When you feel _____ what things do you need to remember to do?

   _____

5. Discuss where, when, and why you most often "feel" this way.

   _____

6. Explain where you can put your symbol so that it will help you make positive choices.

   _____

Additional Suggestions / Considerations

1. Use a straw or toothpick to make a hole in the symbol (prior to drying) if the student wants to hang it using string or ribbon.
2. Prior to drying, students can engrave the symbol with words or pictures using a toothpick.
3. If desired, once it is dry, the symbol can be decorated using paint or markers. Additional embellishments (feathers, gems, sequins) can be glued to the symbol.
4. Students may desire to make more than one to have in different places.
5. Encourage students to be creative with the placement of their object. For example, if the difficulty most often occurs at school, one could make a pencil topper symbol or create a small pendant that can be worn on a bracelet or a magnet that could be hung in ones' locker, etc.

What Does This Mean?

Directions:
Discuss what each of the following symbols represent and/or prompt people to do.

_____

_____

_____

_____

_____

_____

_____

_____

_____

_____

_____

_____

Lesson 18: Seed Planted

Overview

Students will process how our thoughts affect our feelings and our choices while learning about the principles of plant growth.

Objectives

- Students will identify thoughts that lead to negative feelings and choices.
- Students will understand how positive or truth-thoughts help build a solid foundation for more positive feelings and choices.
- Students will identify ways to reframe their "unhealthy soil" (unhealthy thoughts).

Materials

- Small cups or empty water bottles with the tops cut off
- Potting soil
- Dirt with rocks, sticks, trash in it (soil not suitable for growing things)
- Seeds
- Water

Procedures

1. Show students the unhealthy soil. Begin a discussion about the condition of the soil. Encourage students to predict how good this soil will be for growing healthy plants. Make sure they point out specific reasons the soil will be unhealthy. For example, they may note that the rocks or trash might block the roots from growing.
2. Show students the healthy soil and allow them to discuss the properties of the healthy soil. Again, make sure they highlight specific examples that demonstrate the soil is healthy. For example, they may comment about how dark (nutrient rich) the soil appears or that the soil is free from sticks/rocks/trash and other obstructions.
3. Lead a discussion about how our brains are similar to the soil. Point out that when we allow our brains (soil) to become polluted with negative and/or untrue thoughts, they can become obstructions to making good decisions and having more positive feelings. It is important to make sure our minds are as nutrient rich as possible. To achieve this, sometimes we have to weed out negative thoughts and replace them with more

positive thoughts or more truthful thoughts. *Example: "When you are having a problem understanding a new math concept, you may have the thought, "I can't do this." Repeating this thought over and over may lead you to decide to stop trying at all, so you give up. If you were to train your brain to make a more truthful statement such as, "This is hard, but with help I am determined to learn how to do it." This more truthful and positive statement helps motivate you to continue instead of feeling hopeless and giving up."*

4. Allow students to pick the soil they want and help them plant the seed(s) you have. As students are potting and planting their seed, engage them in a conversation about other necessary ingredients for growth of the plant (sunlight, water, etc.). Make the connection that just making sure the seed is planted in healthy soil does not always mean the outcome will be positive. Just like in our lives, having healthy thoughts alone is not sufficient by itself to lead us to more positive thoughts and choices. While it does provide us the best foundation, we must have discipline and work hard to provide the nourishment that will continue to ensure success. *Example: "Just saying to yourself over and over that you can do something, does not automatically ensure you can do it. You must practice and continue to make a good effort toward reaching the goal or completing the task."*

5. Encourage students to share negative thoughts they struggle with. Guide them to reframe the negative thought into a more positive or truthful statement.

Discussion Questions and Prompts

1. Real soil can become unhealthy and not suitable for growing things. In what ways do you think our minds/thoughts can become unhealthy and end up leading us to make poor choices or have negative feelings?

2. When you have negative thoughts, what can you do to try to start "weeding" them out of your brain?

3. What other things do you need, along with more positive and truthful statements, to help you make more positive choices and feelings?

4. Practice reframing one of your negative thoughts.

Lesson 19: Flowing and Growing

Overview

Students will create a lava bottle to serve as a visual reminder to relax and focus on the things that they can control.

Objectives

- Students will identify areas of their lives that they can control.
- Students will process the difficulties of dealing with life stressors while trying to remain calm and at peace.
- Students will practice relaxation techniques.

Materials

- Empty water bottle
- Vegetable oil
- Water (mixed with your choice of food coloring)
- ** *Optional: seltzer tablets cut into quarters*
- ** *Optional: **Calming Waves** activity sheet (can be done in addition to the lava bottle experiment or in lieu of the water bottle experiment)*

Lesson 19: Flowing and Growing (CONTINUED)

Procedures

1. Engage students in a discussion about how sometimes it feels that life is just out of control. Include relevant examples for your students such as: maybe your grades are terrible, you seem to be arguing all the time with your parents, you and your best friend are not speaking, or you had to quit the sport's team because you could not afford the fees. Highlight that when these things continue to happen, we often begin feeling defeated, angry, and/or hopeless. The weight of these difficulties seems to drag us down and our brain becomes polluted with thoughts that tell us things like, "It will never get better," or "There is nothing that you can do." Encourage students to share times they have been in similar circumstances.

2. Pour vegetable oil into the empty bottle—fill it about 3/4 of the way full. Explain that when facing difficult circumstances, we often want to jump in and fix the problem or we feel hopeless because we cannot. Point out that in all circumstances, there are clearly things we can control and things we cannot. Pour the water into the bottle—leave about 1 inch of the bottle empty. What happened? Allow students to respond. Highlight how they clearly separated. Make the point again how that response is relevant to life—there are things we can control, and things we cannot—a very clear separation. Now, shake the bottle and explain that sometimes, our thoughts and feelings get all mixed up in the process. Give examples of some common thoughts/feelings when facing tough situations (my life is terrible, things will always be this way, I am so angry I am going to explode, they better do what I say, etc.). Explain that when this happens, we could benefit if we could stop, calm ourselves, and get into a more peaceful state of mind. Allow students to observe what happens after the bottle sits for a minute.

3. Encourage students to discuss what happens when we try to relax and/or achieve a more peaceful state of mind. State that one of the most important concepts to achieve peace during the chaos is defining what we can or cannot control in a circumstance. Give several scenarios for the students to work through. *Examples: "You and your best friend are not speaking. What can you control in this situation? You just heard the latest gossip being spread around about you. What can you control? You failed the last two tests in class. Your progress report is going home today and you were already grounded because of poor grades. What can you control?"*

4. Once students understand the concept of defining what they control, explain that just having the knowledge does not always make the feelings/thoughts go away. Drop 1/4 of a seltzer tablet into the bottle. Allow students to observe what happens. Explain how these thoughts and feelings often still get a little mixed up. Explain that when this occurs, it is important to engage in activities/things that encourage calm/peaceful thoughts or help

Lesson 19: Flowing and Growing (CONTINUED)

relaxation. Allow student to brainstorm things that can help them relax or calm their thoughts/feelings (examples: listening to music, writing, art, physical activity/exercise, deep breathing, meditation, quiet time, praying, reading positive thoughts/quotes, enjoying the outdoors, etc.).

5. If using the **Calming Waves** activity sheet, allow students to complete the sheet to serve as reminders of the session. If using in lieu of the lava bottle experiment, engage in the same discussions as previously described. Instead of using the bottle as a visual prompt, just ask students to complete the sheet at the end or at different points during the discussions.

Discussion Questions and Prompts

1. Tell about a time when you have felt defeated, angry, and or hopeless.

_____

_____

2. Sometimes, life circumstances are hard to deal with. Share some thoughts or feelings you have had when you have faced difficult circumstances.

_____

_____

3. When facing difficult circumstances, what can you control?

_____

_____

4. What are some things that help you relax and/or clear your mind?

_____

_____

Calming Waves

Directions: On the first row of waves, write yourself reminders of things you can control in your life. On the second row of waves write relaxation techniques that you think would help you remain calm when facing difficult circumstances.

Lesson 20: Instead of

Overview

Students will create a bowl that holds prompts to reframe negative thoughts and/or feelings.

Objectives

- Students will identify negative thoughts and/or feelings that are pervasive within their minds.
- Students will practice reframing negative thoughts.
- Students will create reframing prompts to help with reframing thoughts in the future.

Materials

- Dough recipe (page 16)
- Paper, cut into small strips for writing
- Pencil

** *Optional: sheet of positive quotes*

Procedures

1. Give students a portion of the dough-large enough to shape a small bowl. Instruct students to shape the dough into a bowl or container/platter. While students are working on shaping the object, discuss how our brains are similar to bowls/containers. Explain that our brains hold and process the thoughts we have. Discuss how sometimes the thoughts can be really good/positive and oftentimes they can be negative. Allow students to share some positive and negative thoughts.

2. Once the bowls/containers have been shaped, place them somewhere to dry. Discuss with students how our thoughts can also affect the way we feel. Allow them to share examples from their own lives. Explain that when we are thinking negative thoughts, we can make an effort to stop them or turn them into more positive thoughts. Allow students to practice changing negative thoughts into positive ones using the following examples:
   - I cannot do this.
   - I will never be good at…
   - No one likes me.
   - I hate myself.
   - I am a failure.
   - Everyone thinks I am terrible.

3. Give the students several pieces of the cut paper and a pencil. Encourage them to write positive thoughts that can replace the negative thoughts they have. You may want to have a few sheets of positive quotes for students to use as well. Keep them for the students to place in their bowls/containers once they are dry.

Discussion Questions and Prompts

1. What are some positive thoughts you have had? What are some negative thoughts you have had?

_____

_____

2. Explain how the positive thoughts make you feel. Explain how the negative thoughts make you feel.

_____

_____

3. When you are having negative thoughts, what can you do to replace them with more positive thoughts?

_____

_____

Additional Suggestion

• You can extend this idea into another session by allowing students to paint/decorate their containers. You can continue the idea of reframing/replacing thoughts.

Lesson 21: Stress Reliever

Overview

After making slime, students will explore and document ways that one could squeeze or manipulate the slime in ways that provide a release to built up emotion or stress.

Objectives

- Students will process the difficulties that occur when feeling stressed.
- Students will practice ways that help one appropriately release stress.

Materials

- A stick than can be bent and broken
- Slime recipe (page 45)
- Small plastic bags (if you are going to allow students to take the slime with them)
- Copy of **Slimy Mess** activity sheet for each student

Procedures

1. Engage students in a discussion about what happens when they feel stressed. Students may need you or others participating in the session to define stress. It can be explained in terms of pressure. Use a stick and demonstrate how when you put stress/pressure on the stick, it must change. Show how it begins to bend. Allow students to discuss what they observed. Highlight how stress in our lives feels like pressure. Prompt students to discuss what happens when we do not effectively deal with the stress in our lives. Demonstrate by placing lots of stress/pressure on the stick until it eventually breaks. Discuss how unlike the stick, we do not actually break in two pieces, but we can become so preoccupied with the stress we are unable to focus and concentrate on the things that need our attention.

2. Allow students to make slime using the recipe. Once the slime is created, distribute copies of **Slimy Mess**. Ask students to observe what happens when stress is put on the slime. Instruct them to squeeze it really hard. Have them write the results on their paper. Ask them to make connections between what they observed and their own lives.

3. Discuss how people react differently to stress. Use the analogy of a roller coaster. Naturally, going up and down at really fast speeds produces stress on a person. Some people on the coaster are tense, making grueling faces, or mercifully grasping the bars. Other people, who face the exact same stressors, are wide-eyed, smiling, and have their hands waving in the air! Ask students, "When you feel stress, how do you usually respond?" Encourage them to give specific examples. Have them write the results on #2 of **Slimy Mess**.

4. Ask students to pick the slime back up. Encourage them to manipulate it, pull it, stretch it, and just be creative with it. As they play with the slime, ask them to think of analogies or ways they could use the slime to help them deal with the stressors in their life. Have them complete the remainder of **Slimy Mess** when they are finished. Some examples:
   - I can squeeze it to release some of the intense feeling.
   - I can remind myself that I will get through this — just like the slime comes out of my hands when I put stress on it.
   - I can find encouragement that even if the slime is torn to pieces, it can still come back together. No matter what happens, I can resume my life.
   - I can use different hands to play with the slime. Sometimes when dealing with stress, I may need the help of others.

Discussion Questions and Prompts

1. What happens when emotions get out of control?

   _____

   _____

2. Tell about a time when you had regrets about losing control of your emotions and/or actions.

   _____

   _____

3. What does it mean to feel stressed?

   _____

   _____

4. What do you do when you feel stressed?

_____

_____

5. What happens if you do not effectively deal with your stress?

_____

_____

6. What are some ways that you can effectively deal with your stress?

_____

_____

7. How can others help you deal with your stress?

_____

_____

Slimy Mess

Follow the instructions above each picture.

Write what happened when you placed stress on the slime.

_____

_____

_____

_____

How do you usually respond when you feel stressed?

_____

_____

_____

_____

On each of the following pictures, write a way in which the slime can help you deal with the stress in your life.

Lesson 22: Devastating Destruction

Overview

Students will process the after effects that can occur when emotions are left unattended or unrestrained. The process of loss will be explored using visual analogies of tornados and/or hurricanes.

Objectives

- Students will be able to identify the effects of emotional outbursts on themselves and others.
- Students will be able to define the concepts of impulsivity, thinking ahead, and taking responsibility for our actions.

Materials

- Aftermath pictures of disasters (tornados, hurricanes, floods, and fires etc.)
- ** *Note: Pictures can be from any source: books, magazines, or online.*
- Copy of **The Aftermath** activity sheet for each student

Procedures

1. Begin the session with a discussion about the effects of disasters. Allow students to look at and discuss the pictures you provided. Explain that when people hear a disaster is lurking, they generally do not get excited about the destruction it is going to cause. If anything, they take precautions to make sure the least amount of damage as possible is done. Give examples of boarding up windows, piling up sandbags, anchoring things to the ground, etc. Say to students, "In our lives, we would benefit from doing the same. What do you think I mean?"

2. Lead into a discussion about how sometimes when we are faced with circumstances, we want to react immediately without thinking. Explain and elaborate about impulsivity. Discuss how when we are faced with these intense circumstances and/or feelings, we need to think about our actions and know that we are responsible for them instead of just impulsively doing what first crosses our brains. Encourage sharing/dialogue among the students.

3. When disasters strike, they usually don't effect just the people in the path. Many others are affected as well. For example, if a family is displaced due to a flood damaged home, that family may go and temporarily stay with another family until they can return home. So

even though the flood did not cause damage to the family they are staying with, it does have effects. Your actions always have effects on others you interact with—regardless if you intended them to or not. Distribute copies of **The Aftermath** and work with the students as they complete the activity. Encourage discussion after each scenario. Encourage students to come up with more scenarios.

4. Ask, "What generally happens shortly after a disaster occurs?" Of course, the clean up and rebuilding process begins. Using **The Aftermath** activity, allow students to discuss ways that clean-up and the rebuilding process could occur by thinking and taking responsibility for one's actions.

Discussion Questions and Prompts

1. When people know a disaster is coming, how do they usually feel? What do they hope the outcome will be? What about when a disaster strikes suddenly with no warning? Do people generally like the effect it leaves?

2. Tell about the aftermath of one of your impulsive outbursts.

3. What does it mean to act impulsively?

4. What does it mean to be responsible for your actions? Share a specific example.

5. You completely blew it—you acted impulsively and said some hurtful things to a friend. What could you do to start repairing the damage?

The Aftermath

Beside each picture, write some possible effects from the situation described.

You heard your friend was gossiping about you. You were furious and immediately told her what was on your mind. Later, you find out she didn't say anything about you.

_____

_____

_____

_____

You studied really hard for a test and made a failing grade. You are taking another test in the same class tomorrow. You decide since it didn't help you last time, you won't study.

_____

_____

_____

_____

You made the sport's team you tried out for. At the first practice the coach points out some areas of improvement. You immediately begin shouting telling him how a fellow team member did worse than you. Out of frustration, you leave the practice.

_____

_____

_____

_____

70

Resiliency Revolution: The Change Process

"Just change your behavior or choices." That sounds easy enough, but the truth is, change is a very difficult process. Motivation, discipline, and encouragement are often needed to initiate and follow through with the change process. In his book, "Succeeding When You're Supposed to Fail," Brafman (2011) asserts that a person's ability to change or overcome, even in the face of adversity, is dependent on factors such as having an internal locus of control, searching out meaning, staying calm, having commitment, giving oneself a break, and allowing oneself to be inspired. In this section, sessions will focus on walking students through the change process, thus igniting a resiliency revolution.

Lesson 23: Brain Beads

Overview

Students will create beads that serve as prompts to remind themselves of the thoughts and actions they identify as necessary to help them face difficult situations and/or have the strength to change.

Objectives

- Students will identify words that encourage and motivate them to overcome difficult life circumstances.
- Students will process their feelings associated with facing difficult situations/choices.
- Students will create beads with the words to serve as prompts in their daily lives.

Materials

- Dough recipe (page 16)
- Fine-tip permanent markers
- Toothpicks
- ** *Optional: String for beading once dried (yarn, leather, kite string, etc.)*
- ** *Optional: **Brain Beading** activity sheet (can replace dough activity)*

Procedures

1. Begin with a general discussion about change. Highlight that change is often hard, regardless of how small the change may be. Encourage students to identify a time they have changed. Encourage them to specifically identify how the change actually occurred. What choices did they have to make? What obstacles did they have to overcome, etc.?

2. Encourage students to share their feelings and thoughts as they went through the process of change. For example, a student may discuss how they were just tired and wanted to give up but on the other hand, they wanted the end result. They may describe this as a war raging inside—a constant battle. As feelings and thoughts are processed, brainstorm ways to combat the thoughts and feelings that keep one from success.

3. Give students a portion of the dough (if skipping the dough activity, proceed with the following discussion, just skip the dough bead exercises). Explain that oftentimes when we are trying to make changes in our lives or we face a difficult circumstance, we need motivation and/or encouragement to keep pressing on. Encourage students to share

how/where they can find this motivation and encouragement. Instruct students to form the dough into round beads. If they want to string them, have them use a toothpick to make a hole for stringing later. After forming, allow the beads to dry (if you prefer to finish this in one session, you can have the beads made and just give them out, and continue the next procedure).

4. Distribute copies of **Brain Beading**. Have students complete the activity. Take opportunities that may arise to continue encouraging students to share their ideas, etc.

5. If students made brain beads, during the next session, continue the discussion and reinforcement. Allow them to decorate their beads using markers with the words or ideas they listed on the **Brain Beading** activity page.

Discussion Questions and Prompts

1. How do you determine when you need to change something in your life?

_____

_____

2. Share a time when you really wanted to quit something but you toughed it out.

_____

_____

3. When you are trying to achieve something and you face an obstacle or a set back, what keeps you motivated to keep trying?

_____

_____

Additional Suggestion

- Consider showing videos or sharing stories of people who have faced great adversity and were able to continue making positive choices despite the circumstances. Allow students to discuss the stories/videos and identify what kept the people motivated to continue the change process.

Brain Beading

Directions: Decorate each bead and write a word on each that motivates and encourages you to keep pushing ahead despite difficult circumstances!

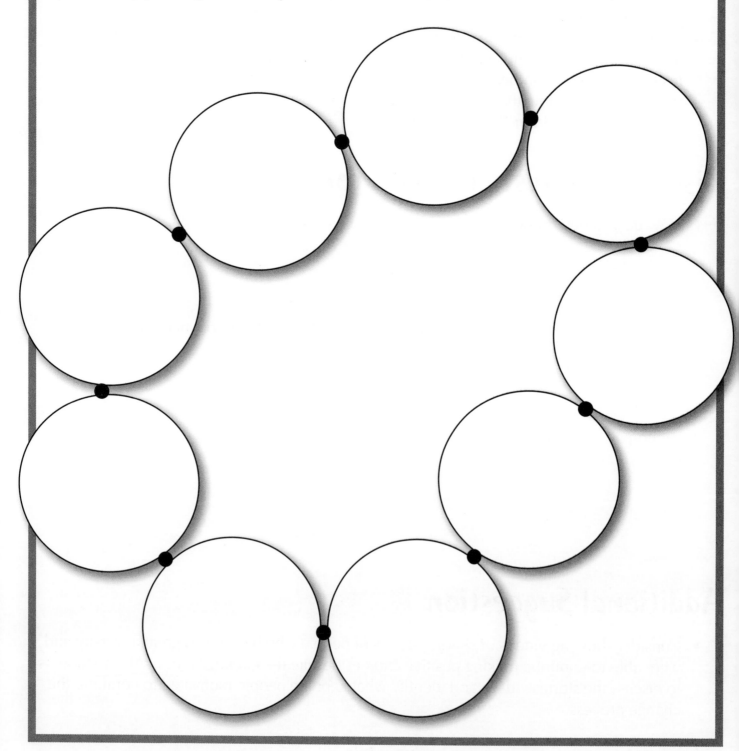

Lesson 24: Rock World

Overview

Students will identify and design rocks that represent challenges/obstacles they must overcome to change an area of their life.

Objectives

- Students will identify obstacles and challenges they face.
- Students will process ways to overcome the obstacles and challenges.
- Students will share stories of successes and failures in overcoming obstacles and challenges.
- Students will create visual rock prompts to remind themselves of things they are trying to overcome.

Materials

- Masking tape or yarn/string
- Paper
- Blindfold
- Rocks
- Paint or permanent markers
- Paper to put under rocks when designing

Procedures

1. Prior to students' arrival, make a lane using the masking tape or the yarn/string. Inside the lane, place pieces of paper randomly down the lane.
2. When students arrive, begin a discussion similar to the following: "Navigating life can sometimes be a difficult task. There are often obstacles and challenges that must be overcome in order to live the life you desire. To demonstrate this process, we will do an activity."
3. Instruct students to walk down the lane without stepping on any of the "obstacles" in the lane. Afterwards, ask the students to give feedback about the ease of the task. Next, blindfold a student and ask them to walk down the lane avoiding the obstacles. Let that student or others try several times to complete the task. At various points, encourage the students to brainstorm ways to make the task easier. Allow them to try out their ideas.

4. Discuss how this activity is similar to life. Explain, "Sometimes, things go smoothly, just like how you were able to navigate the path avoiding the obstacles. Other times, it may seem like we can not catch a break. We constantly run into obstacles and do not really know what to do." Encourage the students to discuss the strategies they used to overcome the obstacles.

5. Allow students to get a few rocks. Prompt students to share some of their successes and failures when facing obstacles/challenges. Allow them to brainstorm some of the current obstacles/challenges they are facing in their lives.

6. Instruct the students to decorate the rocks that represent some of those challenges. For example, one may paint/draw a picture of an A to represent the struggle he/she faces with grades in school; another may paint a black rock that represents the loss of someone significant in their life. Once students are finished designing their rocks, allow them to share with the group what each one represents.

7. After each student shares, encourage the group to brainstorm strategies that can help each other overcome the obstacles and challenges they face.

Discussion Questions and Prompts

1. Share some obstacles and challenges you face in life.

_____

_____

2. Share some failures and successes you have had when facing obstacles/challenges.

_____

_____

3. When facing an obstacle/challenge and you have no clue how to proceed, where do you get direction?

_____

_____

4. What are some strategies you could use to overcome the current obstacles you face?

_____

_____

Lesson 25: Downstream

Overview

Students will design a canoe or boat as change, obstacles, and/or challenges are discussed.

Objectives

- Students will learn some basic principles of canoeing.
- Students will understand that navigating around obstacles often includes failure and having to change strategies.
- Students will practice assessing situations and realizing that a different choice or strategy should be used.

Materials

- Dough recipe (page 16)
- Paper cut into small strips/pieces
** *Optional video clips/pictures of canoeing*

Procedures

1. Discuss some basic principles of canoeing. If you have some video clips/pictures, show these to the students. Discuss these facts:
   - The person in the back steers the direction of the boat.
   - If there is more than one person paddling, both must work together. If they do not, the boat will turn in circles.
   - Balance must be maintained or it will flip over.
   - Trees and other debris can fall into the water and create strainers in the water. These strainers can trap and hold a canoe. If a person is dumped and approaches a strainer, he/she should always try to go over the strainer not under.
   - When paddling a canoe, there are proper and improper ways to take strokes.

2. Make application of the canoe analogy by stating that sometimes in our lives, we need to follow certain strategies and principles to be successful. When canoeing, the person navigating the boat must make certain choices and engage in actions to successfully move the canoe downstream. At any moment on the river, an obstacle can appear and decisions must be made about how to safely navigate. Sometimes, the person makes a mistake and may get dumped into the water! This is the same in our lives. We face challenges and obstacles and sometimes our first response/strategy fails. In these situations, we must consider our choices and possibly adjust our strategy.

3. Give students a portion of the dough and have them create their own canoe/boat. Once created, allow the students to create a river of obstacles. Instruct them to use the paper to create obstacles for the canoe. After a few minutes of play, ask them to consider their own lives and share challenges they face.

4. Actively process the students' obstacles. Help them identify a workable plan to overcome the obstacle. If they have been successful, help them brainstorm other possible strategies to try out. If students are having a difficult time understanding how to change strategies, share the following scenarios and let them decide how to change strategies to be more successful.

   • Juan wanted to make new friends, but has been unsuccessful. No one in class has made an effort to talk to him and at break, he still stands alone. He hopes that tomorrow he will make a new friend.

   • Ava has failed the last two chapter tests. She does not understand why. She has read and reread the material.

   • Anthony always caves into peer pressure when around a certain group of friends. He always tells himself he is going to be strong and say, "No." Hopefully, tonight, he will be strong.

5. Make a point about how changing strategies/choices can be an obstacle in itself. Allow students to consider and discuss this concept as well. Either allow students to take the canoes with them or save the dough for another day.

Discussion Questions and Prompts

1. Share a time you faced a challenge and the action/strategy you used failed. What did you do after the failure?

_____

_____

2. Share a time you successfully overcame a challenge/obstacle. What actions/strategy did you use?

_____

_____

3. Share a time you had to change courses/plans to be successful.

_____

_____

4. Do you think it is possible to get very different results by doing the same thing over and over?

_____

_____

5. Changing course is not that easy to do. Discuss the challenge of making new choices. (For example: It is easy to say, "Find new friends." In reality, how easy is that accomplished?)

_____

_____

Lesson 26: Superhero or Villain?

Overview

Students will create a mask that serves as a talking point about the power of perception.

Objectives

- Students will be able to define perception.
- Students will give an example of how perception can affect them.
- Students will understand how other's perceptions can be different from their own.

Materials

- Copy of **Which is It?** activity sheet or a white half-face mask for each student
- Yarn (if using the activity sheet)
- Markers or paint for decorating
- 1 half-face mask cut out from the **Which is It?** activity sheet or 1 white half-mask

Procedures

1. Show students the half-face mask. Ask them if the mask belongs to a superhero or a villain. Prompt them to discuss how they made their decisions. Introduce the concept of perception. There are several ways to define perception. A good example is: an impression or an understanding based on what one sees or thinks. Continue the discussion while stating, "We make decisions often on our thoughts about something, just like you made a decision about the mask. The truth is the mask could be a villain or a superhero depending on how you perceived the mask."

2. Allow students to design and decorate masks on their own. If using the activity sheet, allow them to cut them out and use yarn for tying. After they are finished, let the students share with the group about their masks—superhero or a villain? Begin a discussion about how sometimes two people can experience the same thing but have completely different feelings/thoughts (perceptions). For example, two people ride a roller coaster—one thinks it was the worst thing ever—the other thinks it is the best thing ever. Hmmm…same coaster—who is right and who is wrong? Each person's experience dictates their perception. While each person has a unique perception, sometimes one's perception can be skewed. For example: One may fear giving a speech in front of a crowd and the

perception of the person is the speech was awful. However, once the crowd began giving feedback, the one who gave the speech began to realize that the speech may not have been that bad (the perception began changing).

3. Instruct students to put on their masks. Explain that we should always be challenging our perceptions. Sometimes, having a different perspective can give us the needed motivation to begin or continue the change process. For example, when we have an experience and others give us different feedback or share different perspectives, we should be willing to take that into consideration. Highlight that when we are trying to overcome obstacles in our life or face difficult circumstances our perceptions may not necessarily be the best. Other people in our lives may offer feedback or share their perceptions to help one have a more accurate perception. Allow students to discuss times when they have shifted their perception regarding something when they received different feedback. Encourage students to take the masks to serve as reminders to them to always consider differing perceptions.

Discussion Questions and Prompts

1. What is perception?

   _____

2. Tell about a time when your perception of an event was different than someone else's.

   _____

3. Has your perception about something ever changed? Share the experience.
   What prompted the change?

   _____

4. How does your perception effect you when you are trying to experience change in your life?

   _____

5. Many times, we are quick to shut someone out of our lives because we "perceive" them a certain way. Do you think it might be worth trying to understand them before making that decision? Why or why not?

Which is It?

Directions: Decorate and cut out this mask.

Lesson 27: What Motivates Me?

Overview

Students will begin to process and explore personal motivation as they observe objects and pictures.

Objectives

- Students will understand the concept of motivation.
- Students will identify sources of motivation.
- Students will process some of the challenges with staying motivated.

Materials

- Pictures (in print or digital), quotes and/or video clips of scenes in which people are overcoming obstacles or talking about motivation
- Magazines
- Markers
- Glue
- Paper or poster board

Procedures

1. Begin the session by telling students they are going to write, "I am going to learn about motivation today," 30 times. Tell them to get a pencil/paper and get ready. As they are preparing, give them a few seconds, and then ask them how they felt about the task. Ask if anyone is excited about the task. Now, ask how they would feel about the assignment if you offered them $20 for completing the task. Encourage discussion about why the attitude/feeling changed. Lead them to defining the concept of motivation (a simple definition of motivation: a reason to act).

2. Show students a picture/video prompt or quote. Lead a discussion about what is taking place. Highlight the challenge/obstacles that may be portrayed. Encourage students to identify how the person may stay motivated to keep going despite the difficulties they face. For example: You could have a picture of Kyle Maynard completing a task. Kyle Maynard has no arms or legs but climbs mountains, fights professionally, and is a motivational speaker. Show students a few more pictures, videos, or quotes and repeat the discussion.

3. Encourage students to share about times in which they became motivated to do something. Explain that oftentimes when we are trying to change or tackle a new or difficult task, we lose motivation and want to quit. Point out that during these times, it is helpful to identify sources to go to in an effort to help increase one's motivation. Prompt students to identify things/circumstances that decrease their motivation. Allow students to process strategies to keep this from happening or to regain/strengthen their motivation level.

4. Give students a piece of paper or poster board. Explain that you want them to design a motivational poster for themselves. If you want, show some examples of motivational posters (a quick online search will populate several examples). Have magazines for them to cut out pictures. You can also have quotes for them to use. Have markers available for drawing or adding more decoration. Encourage students to hang the poster somewhere that will help provide them motivation when they are in need.

   **Note: If you have a bulletin board, you may want students to design a motivational bulletin board for your office or the school.

Discussion Questions and Prompts

1. What is motivation?

_____

2. What keeps people motivated?

_____

3. Tell about a time you did not want to do something, but then you found a source a motivation and completed the task.

_____

4. When you are unmotivated, what are sources of motivation for you?

_____

5. What circumstances/events tend to decrease your motivation? What can you do when this happens?

_____

Lesson 28: Mold Me

Overview

Provide students with an understanding of how changing behavior is a process while creating various objects from dough.

Objectives

- Students will understand that behavioral changes are often difficult and require lots of time and practice.
- Students will identify one area in which they would like to make some behavioral changes.
- Students will create a behavior goal.
- Students will begin developing an action plan to start practicing as they work toward completion of their goal.

Materials

- Dough recipe (page 16)
- A copy of the **Mold Me** activity sheet for each student.
- ** *Optional: cookie cutters, dough molds, or gelatin molds*

Procedures

1. Give each student some dough that is shaped in the form of a ball.
2. Discuss what would need to happen to turn the ball of dough into something else. Highlight the fact it would have to be "molded" or "made" into something else.
3. Call out objects and have students create them using the dough. Allow the use of molds during the first round (if available). Then, ask them to create the objects without molds.
4. After a few rounds, make the objects to be created progressively harder (examples: a snake, a heart, a bird nest, a person, a cat, etc.)
5. Begin linking the activity with the objectives by engaging in discussion questions 1-6.
6. Explain that change is a process—just like you have to mold the dough to create something new, we all have to "mold ourselves" when we want to act in a new way. Discuss or role play some age-appropriate examples. Highlight the fact that change is generally not an easy thing to do—it requires lots of work!
7. Give each student a copy of the **Mold Me** worksheet and continue with discussion as prompted on the worksheet.

Lesson 28: Mold Me (CONTINUED)

Discussion Questions and Prompts

1. Think about what happened when you began molding new objects. Were some things easier than others to make? Give examples.

   _____

   _____

2. Which was easier—making creations from the molds or on your own? Why? Did the mold (the plan) help you create the object with a little less struggle? Do you think having a plan would help you accomplish change in your life?

   _____

   _____

3. Have you ever tried to change anything about yourself? If so, what?

   _____

   _____

4. Was the change you tried to make easy or hard? Give examples.

   _____

   _____

5. When you realize that the change is sometimes hard, what do you do then? (Do you give up, do you try something else?) Give specific examples. When you tried to make the cat did your first plan work? What did you change or what could you have done differently?

   _____

   _____

6. Why do you think it is hard to change?

   _____

   _____

Mold Me

· ·

Think about what you would like to change about yourself. Complete statements 1 and 2.

1. I would like to start _____.

2. I would like to stop _____.

In the space below, write or draw a picture of your goal.

MY GOAL

Think about what you will try first in an effort to help you change and meet your goal. Draw or write the steps in the box below.

ACTION PLAN

FOLLOW UP

After 1 week how are you doing?

☐ **I am doing great—I need to keep following this plan!**
☐ **I have not done as well as I wanted, but overall, it is working.**
☐ **It hasn't worked at all—I need a new plan.**
☐ **Other:** _____

_____

Lesson 29: Trash It

Overview

Students will create a trash can to throw away faulty thinking and actions that do not produce desired results.

Objectives

- Students will identify a goal they want to work towards that requires some change to accomplish.
- Students will identify barriers in their thinking and actions that may prevent the desired results.

Materials

- A shoe box or empty 2-liter/large bottle (if you are working with a large group, you may consider doing more than one)
- Paper for covering box or bottle
- Scissors
- Tape
- Markers
- Copies of **Trash It** activity sheet for each student
- ** *Note: This activity sheet can be done in conjunction or in lieu of the trash can activity.*

Procedures

1. Instruct students that they are going to create a trash can for faulty thinking and actions. Allow students to design the trash can. Let them tape the paper around the bottle/box and decorate it.
2. Once the trash can is complete, lead a discussion that helps students identify a goal they would like to accomplish that will require some change on their part. Help guide them to make sure their goals are specific, realistic, and attainable within a reasonable amount of time. Distribute copies of the **Trash It** activity sheet. Allow them to write their goal on the sheet.

3. Discuss what specific actions/thoughts will be needed in order to achieve the goals. Have students write these at the bottom of the *Trash It* activity sheet. As students brainstorm ideas, write them on a board/paper for further exploration. Once students come up with some ideas, go back through the ideas and discuss some thoughts/actions that could hinder success. As students brainstorm these, have them write them on strips of paper and put them in the trash can. They can also write them on the trash can picture on the activity sheet.

4. Inform students that you will continue to check in with them regarding the progress toward the goal. Let them know that as thoughts/actions appear that hinder success, they can always trash them and recycle them into thoughts/actions that help promote success. For example: One may have a goal to be more organized. After using several things one day when he/she is tired, he/she has the thought, "I am too tired. I'll put the stuff up tomorrow." This thought can be recycled into a more success-promoting thought, "I am tired, but I am going to take a few minutes and get this done because it is important to me." Use other examples that are relevant to the students' situations and concerns.

Discussion Questions and Prompts

1. What is a short-term goal you would like to achieve that would require you to make a change in your thoughts and/or actions?

_____

_____

2. What are some thoughts/actions that hinder your success when you try to make changes?

_____

_____

3. What are some positive thoughts/actions that promote success when you try to make changes?

_____

_____

4. When you seem to be bombarded with negative thoughts/actions, what are some things you can do to help recycle your thoughts/actions?

_____

Trash It

Directions: In the space above the trash can, write a goal you would like to work toward that requires some change on your part. On the picture, write thoughts/actions down that will not help you produce the desired change. On the space at the bottom, write thoughts and actions that will help you produce the change.

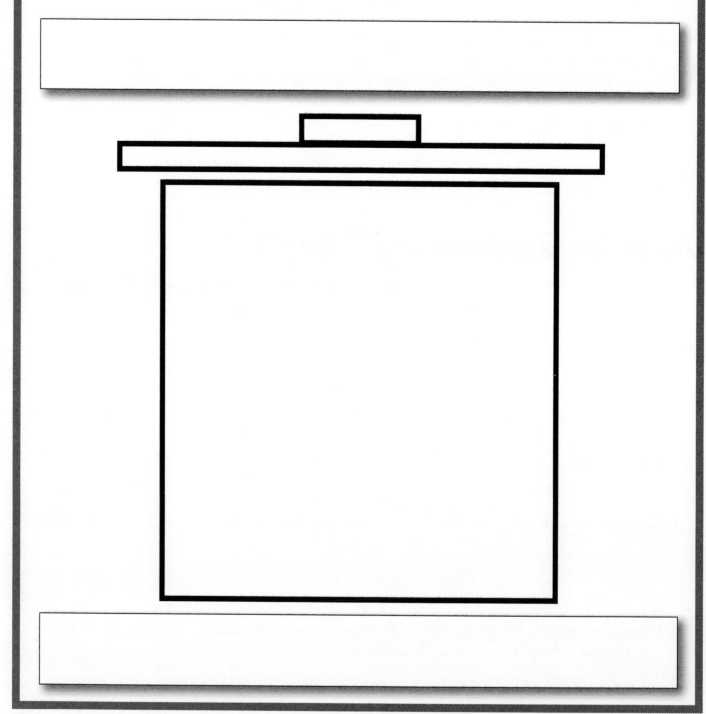

Lesson 30: Impaired Thinking

Overview

Students construct materials in a bottle that represent how messed up our thinking/perception can be during times of change, conflict, or emotional turmoil.

Objectives

- Students will identify thinking that is counter-productive to positive change.
- Students will identify strategies to help foster more positive thoughts.
- Students will challenge their own faulty thoughts.

Materials

- A pair of sunglasses/reading glasses that are really dirty, scratched, or smudged
- Empty plastic bottles (water/soda)
- ** *Note: If doing this for a large group, you may want to do just 1 or 2. If you are using this with an individual or small group, you may want one for each person.*
- Rice or sand
- Small objects that will fit in the bottle (pennies, paper clips, buttons, small keys, small toys, etc.)

Procedures

1. Begin the session with the dirty glasses on. Ask students how well they think you can see. Lead a short discussion about why they think your vision may be impaired. How can we make it clearer? Why does it matter if my vision is messed up? Lead into a discussion about how just like our vision can become impaired, so can our thinking. Explain that when we are experiencing adversity or when we are emotionally overwhelmed, we may get a little distorted with our thinking. *Example: "You just had a major argument with your friend and you walk into class and your teacher gives you a difficult assignment. You may not be able to fully concentrate because your thinking is a little distorted. You may be thinking about the argument and therefore, only hearing parts of the instructions. By the time you are to begin the assignment, you have no clue what to do. You know you have the ability to complete the assignment but you can not keep you thoughts clear enough to think about it."* Our thinking can also become distorted/clouded when we experience failure or setbacks. Encourage students to share their thoughts and feelings when they have

experienced failure/setbacks. Highlight some of the thoughts shared and point out that under different circumstances you may not have those same thoughts/perceptions.

2. Show students the small objects you have. You may want to list them on a board or card so they can be referred to later. Pour a little sand/rice in the bottle and drop an object or two in, pour in more sand/rice, add another object or two. Repeat until it is almost full and all the objects are in the bottle (leave about 1/2 inch at the top so the sand/rice can be manipulated). Point out that all of the listed objects are in the bottle and they can be sure they are there. Give them the bottle and allow them to manipulate it to try to find the items. When they have trouble finding an object, use this as a talking point. Explain that before the items were put into the rice/sand, we could clearly see them. But now that we have added the other items in the bottle, we have trouble seeing them as clearly. This is just like our thinking. It sometimes gets harder to think clearly or have the right perception when our thinking is crowded.

3. Point out that one of the times that our thinking can become impaired is when we are trying to make changes in our lives and with our choices. Sometimes, we immediately reject the idea that we can improve our situation. Have you ever been complaining about something and someone offers a suggestion? Sometimes, we immediately say things like, "Nothing will work. It will always be this way." For some reason, when we are facing certain situations, our thoughts do not always encourage change or the most positive thinking. What can we do when we recognize we have distorted thinking? Guide students to identify strategies to help produce more positive thoughts as they process and share ideas.

Discussion Questions and Prompts

1. How can your thinking become clouded or impaired?

_____

2. When is impaired thinking most likely to occur for you? Share an example.

_____

3. What strategies do you think you could try when you experience impaired thinking?

_____

4. Who is someone you trust to process your thoughts with when you feel you may have impaired thinking/perceptions?

_____

Lesson 31: The Author of My Own Story

Overview

Students will make chalk as they process the concept of how their choices define who they are as a person.

Objectives

- Students will understand the concept of resiliency.
- Students will identify how they can be the author of their own story instead of their circumstances and/or other people.
- Students will make chalk to serve as a visual reminder of the session.

Materials

- Cardboard tube (toilet paper, paper towel rolls)
- Scissors
- Duct tape
- Freezer paper or wax paper
- Container for mixing
- Tempera paint
- 1 cup water
- 1 1/2 cups Plaster of Paris
- Spoon for mixing

CHALK RECIPE

Cut cardboard tubes to the desired length. Tape off one end of the tube. Insert freezer/wax paper inside the tube to prevent sticking. Mix 3 tablespoons of tempera paint with 1 cup of water. Add the Plaster of Paris to the mixture. Stir until mixed thoroughly. Fill tubes with the mixture. The chalk can be removed from the tube in approximately 1 hour (squeeze the tubes to check for hardness. Allow chalk to cool for 24 hours before use.

Lesson 31: The Author of My Own Story

(CONTINUED)

Procedures

1. Have a general discussion about the role of authors. Point out that authors decide what happens in stories. They make decisions and choices that direct the plot of the story. Ask students to discuss their own lives. Who is the author of your story? Encourage them to explain why they chose the answer they did.

2. Explain that while we are the authors of our stories (lives) for the most part, sometimes the outcomes we expect are not what we get. *Example: "You may have practiced every day to make a sports team. But when tryouts came, you were cut the first day. If you were writing your complete story, more than likely you would have been on the team. In honesty, these are the times you actually do get to be the author of your own story."* In times of adversity, challenge, and failure we are all faced with many choices: quit, keep trying, change strategies, throw fits, whine, withdraw, etc. The ability to bounce back from adversity or problems is called resiliency. Encourage students to share a time they have faced a circumstance and shown resilience. You may need to share an example or two for them to fully understand. Share, "When a person is not resilient we often say they have become a product of their circumstance or environment. What do you think this means?"

3. Ask students to share some of the current challenges, obstacles, and adversity they face or see themselves facing in the future. Ask, "What choices can you make in these circumstances to demonstrate resiliency?" Encourage students to brainstorm several ideas.

4. Present the materials for the chalk recipe. Explain that you are now all going to make chalk to serve as a visual reminder that when facing adverse situations, we can choose to be an author of our story. Lead the students through the creation of the chalk. You can highlight that when they make a choice and it does not work out like they want, they can erase it (like they can erase chalk), and start over with a new choice.

Lesson 31: The Author of My Own Story

Discussion Questions and Prompts

1. Who is the author of your story (life)? Explain your answer.

2. Who determines the outcome of your story?

3. What happens when you intend on one thing happening and something else occurs that you did not expect?

4. What makes a person resilient?

5. What does it mean to be a victim of one's circumstance? For example: A student may live in an environment in which no one has graduated high school, and they do not value education. When high school becomes a challenge, no one is surprised when he/she drops out.

6. In the above situation, how could the person show resiliency?

Lesson 32: What State are you in?

Overview

Students will process concepts of change by understanding, observing, and experimenting with different forms of matter.

Objectives

- Students will explore different states of matter.
- Students will identify how change often occurs in different phases of our lives.
- Students will discuss strategies to begin the change process.

Materials

- One batch of **What is this Stuff?** (made prior to session)
- Examples of different states of matter (liquids, solids, gases)

WHAT IS THIS STUFF? RECIPE

2 cups corn starch   1 cup water
bowl   *optional food coloring

Mix the corn starch, water, and food coloring together in a bowl. The mixture will "feel" difficult to stir. Just turn the spoon slowly. Efforts to rush this process will not be successful!

Procedures

1. Begin the session by showing and teaching a little about states of matter-liquids, solids, gases (and plasmas if ages permit). Show students examples and have them identify the state of matter. Once students understand the concept, explain that matter can change states depending on what happens around it. Use water for an example. The most common form of water is liquid. Allow students to identify where they can observe water in the liquid state. Then explain when water is exposed to temperatures below 32 degrees Fahrenheit, it freezes and becomes ice (a solid). Allow students to identify where they can observe water in the solid state. When water reaches the boiling point of 212 degrees Fahrenheit, it begins changing to steam (a gas). Allow students to identify where they can observe water in the gaseous state. Apply these examples by pointing out that we often

must change, just as these substances changed, as their situations did. Sometimes, the change is welcomed and other times it is just necessary.

2. Show students **What is This Stuff?**. Explain that this substance actually has the properties of a liquid and a solid. Pour a small portion of the substance into another container to demonstrate the liquid state. After that demonstration, have students take their fists and quickly tap the substance. It feels/acts like a solid. Their fists will not penetrate the substance. Make application by stating that sometimes when facing circumstances and situations we can be like this stuff. We do not really have an idea of what state we should be in. We have no clue if we should continue the way we are, making the same choices or if we should start the change process and make different choices. How do you determine when you should begin the change process? Encourage students to actively discuss this concept sharing specific examples from their personal experience.

3. Lead the discussion to focus on strategies that can be helpful when beginning the change process (examples: setting goals, finding people to help guide and offer feedback, finding sources of motivation and encouragement, having a specific plan, evaluating the plan, having options in case one plan does not produce the desired results, etc.). Summarize what has been discussed during the session.

Discussion Questions and Prompts

1. Share an example of a time you had to change due to your circumstance or situation. What actions did you have to take?

_____

2. What emotions do you experience when you face having to change?

_____

3. How do you know a change is needed in your life?

_____

4. What are some strategies to use when beginning the change process?

_____

Lesson 33: Why Does This Keep Happening?

Overview

Students will experience and feel the absurdity of repeating an action and expecting something different to happen.

Objectives

- Students will experience the absurdity of repeating an action and expecting different results.
- Students will role play scenarios to assess what needs to happen in order to change the outcome.

Materials

- Copy of **Lights-Go Off!** activity sheet for every student

Procedures

1. Begin the session by asking a student to turn the lights off. Instruct him/her to turn them off by saying, "Light off," or by clapping. Once he/she does the action and the lights do not turn off, instruct him/her to try it again using the same action. Continue this process several times. Comment occasionally with statements such as, "It will work out this time." "I bet this time will be different." Once the process has been repeated and becomes ridiculous, ask the students why the lights did not go off. Explain that while this seems like a simple and ridiculous example, it often mirrors our choices in life. We do something and do not like the results. So what do we do then? We keep repeating the same action expecting something different to happen. For example: We want to make good grades but do not study and do poorly on tests, or we want our parents to trust us but we continue to lie over little things. Explain that sometimes, repeating an action is justified. Just because you fail once does not mean that what you are doing will not work at all. However, after a few repeated attempts it should become evident a new course of action is warranted!

2. Allow students to role play and/or discuss the following scenarios. Highlight the choices made and the results. Allow students to come up with new strategies and role play/discuss the results. Feel free to come up with relevant scenarios for your students.
   - **Desired Outcome: Have strong relationships with friends**
     Sophie and Jannette are friends. One day, Sophie shares with Jannette something she does not want others to know. Jannette has every intention to keep the information between

them. However, two days later, Jannette is with her other friend. While talking, she shares what Sophie told her. Several days later, Sophie confronts her, Jannette apologizes and promises it will not happen again. One month later, Sophie shares something personal with Jannette. Again, Jannette chose to share it with her other friend and told her not to tell. Of course, that friend tells one other person and so on. This gets back to Sophie...

- **Desired Outcome: A good reputation**

  Austin wants others to respect and look up to him. On the football field, he is a star player. However, he often misses practices and downgrades others on the team when they make errors. In class, he lies about doing his assignments and often cheats...

- **Desired Outcome: Save money**

  Jarvis really wants to save his money in hopes of one day buying a car. He earns money by completing chores at home and doing odd jobs for others. He once was able to save $75. However, a new video game was released that he wanted really bad. He purchased it for $54. The next month, he earned $25. He used $14.50 to go out to eat with some of his friends. Over the next 3 months, he earned $90 but spent $7 at a fast food restaurant, $36 at the mall, and $4 at a store buying snacks. Today, he counted his money and could not believe he only had $74.50 of the $190 he had earned.

3. Distribute copies of **Lights-Go Off!** activity sheet. Have students complete the sheet to serve as a reminder of today's session. Encourage them to discuss their answers and brainstorm with you or the group different strategies/actions they can try.

Discussion Questions and Prompts

1. Share about a time you repeated an action hoping the next time would produce different results.

   _____

   _____

2. When you recognize you are in a pattern of repeating the same action but expecting different results, what should you do?

   _____

   _____

3. If you can not seem to come up with different strategies/actions who could help you come up with some ideas?

   _____

Lights—Go Off!

As a reminder of our session today, on the light bulb write down actions that you have been repeating expecting to get different results.

On the small lightbulbs below, write down new actions that you could try to see if they produce a more desired outcome.

Identity Formation

Students today face increasing pressure to conform to the status quo of their current peer group. Forming a solid identity can help students gain the confidence they need to withstand the pressure to conform and to be the person they desire.

Lesson 34: Putting it all Together

Overview

Students will design a puzzle that is a visual reminder of core values and/or attitudes they want to display with their lives.

Objectives

- Students will identify values or attitude they want to display with their lives.
- Students will process the actions that define the identified values/beliefs.
- Students will define how to make situations right when their actions have conveyed the opposite of what they desire.

Materials

- Cardstock (cut 8½ x 11 sheets into halves or fourths depending on the size of your group)
- Markers
- Scissors
- 1 copy of *Putting it all Together-Character Traits* list

Procedures

1. Start a discussion about what character traits/values/attitudes students want to display with their lives. If students are having a difficult time coming up with words, offer some suggestions to get them started or display the *Putting it all Together-Character Traits* list. As students are brainstorming, ask them to define the words they choose.

2. Distribute cardstock paper and ask students to creatively write their words on the paper and decorate it anyway they want. Explain that the paper will be made into a puzzle later. As students engage in the activity, continue allowing them to discuss and process the words they have chosen.

3. Once students are finished designing their paper, ask them to consider what specific actions are necessary for them to display these traits with their lives. For example: A student may have chosen dependable as one of his/her words. For someone to be dependable, he or she must follow through with commitments, be there when others need him/her, and meet and/or exceed expectations/rules. Encourage sharing of many examples.

(CONTINUED)

4. Instruct students to cut their paper into puzzle pieces. Allow them a minute or two to complete this task. Explain that while we desire certain traits to define who we are, we often fail. Just like you cut through some of the words on your paper to make a puzzle, you are sometimes going to mess up and display the opposite of what you really desire. Somehow, you have to figure out how to get it back together. Allow students some time to put their puzzle together.

5. Encourage students to share examples of how to make situations right when they make mistakes. You may offer some relevant scenarios to get them talking and thinking. *Example: "You really desire to be kind to others. However, one day you said some pretty hurtful things to someone else. What can make this right?"* Encourage students to think beyond just saying "I'm sorry." Share with students, "'I'm sorry' is a good start but you have the opportunity when you mess up to model to others ways to make things right. For example, you could say: "I really messed up when I said… as a matter of fact, I was thinking about you and really wanted you to know that you are good at… Please forgive me for the words I said, I am going to try really hard not to repeat this in future." If you aren't comfortable having this conversation, you can write a letter." Explain that facing our mistakes and making it right with other people is very hard but a highly noble thing to do.

Discussion Questions and Prompts

1. What characteristics/values/attitudes do you want to characterize your life? What words would you like others to use when describing you? Why did you choose those specific words?

2. What specific actions are necessary on your part to convey those characteristics/values/attitudes?

3. What happens when your actions have conveyed the opposite of what you desire?

4. When you have messed up, what can you to do make it right?

Putting it all Together— Character Traits

Active
Adventurous
Affectionate
Ambitious
Bossy
Brave
Brilliant
Bully
Calm
Charismatic
Clever
Clumsy
Childish
Cold-hearted
Compassionate
Competitive
Conceited
Concerned
Confident
Cooperative
Courageous
Critical
Cruel
Daring
Dependable

Determined
Dishonest
Disrespectful
Eager
Easy-going
Efficient
Enthusiastic
Fair
Faithful
Friendly
Funny
Generous
Gentle
Greedy
Hopeful
Humorous
Imaginative
Immature
Impulsive
Independent
Intelligent
Kind
Lazy
Logical
Lovable

Loyal
Mature
Mean
Obedient
Observant
Peaceful
Persistent
Pleasant
Polite
Reliable
Respectful
Responsible
Selfish
Sensitive
Sincere
Smart
Sneaky
Snobbish
Stingy
Sweet
Thoughtful
Trustworthy
Warmhearted
Wise

Lesson 35: Solid Foundation

Overview

Students will create a structure using straws and tape. Trials will be conducted to see how much weight the structure can hold. Parallels will be made with the importance of living life with a solid purpose instead of going through life aimlessly.

Objectives

- Students will understand the difference between living with a purpose and living without purpose.
- Students will learn how to assess structures and determine what could be done to make them stronger.
- Students will create a personal purpose statement.

Materials

- Pack of straws (may need several packs depending on the size of the group)
- Tape
- Objects for weight (any random things around your office or you can purchase packs of candy—they stack well and add weight)
- Random objects for purpose discussion (See procedure #1)
- Copy of **Solid Foundation-Purpose** activity sheet for each student

Procedures

1. Begin a discussion about the purpose of things. Have a few examples of random objects (paper clips, paper, book, pencil, duct tape, etc.) Show students an object and have them discuss the purpose of the object. As students discuss the purpose, challenge them to come up with other uses/purposes of the object. For example, a paper clip can be used to clip things together but it can also be used as a hanger for decorations. Repeat this until you have shown each object or until you need to move on.
2. Explain to students they have a task to complete. Divide students into small groups, if there are large numbers of students. Give them the straws and tape and tell them it is their job to build a structure to hold weight. Tell them when they are done, weight will be added to the structure to determine its strength. Allow students to complete the task.

3. As groups finish, test the structures by adding the weight. As this is done, allow the group to discuss the properties that appear to make the structures stronger or weaker. Allow them an opportunity to make changes to their structures and retry to the tests.

4. Make connections between the activity and the topic by pointing out that the purpose of the object was to hold weight. What if I just told you to build a structure but not that it would hold weight? Would that have changed your design? Why or why not? Point out that generally when we know the purpose of something we make decisions based on that purpose. Think about your life. Have you ever given thought to what your purpose may be? Most successful businesses create purpose statements that drive the company. The purpose statement helps guide the decision making process for the company. Do you have a clue what the purpose statement for Coca Cola© may be? "To refresh the world...To inspire moments of optimism and happiness...To create value and make a difference." (Quote extracted from www.coca-colacompany.com) Allow students to discuss how this purpose statement might guide some of the decisions of the company.

5. Just like objects and companies have purpose, so do you. Your life impacts those around you on a daily basis. Having an understanding of your purpose can help guide the decisions you make. Distribute copies of **Solid Foundation-Purpose** activity sheet and allow students to complete the activity. Encourage students to consider their purpose and alter it in the future as they need to. Explain that as they grow older they may experience new things and understand their purpose more fully. For example, duct tape was originally created to seal duct vents together. Think of all the uses of it now. Years ago, no one would have thought to use it to decorate items. Share, "So, as you go throughout life, consider the purpose for which your life serves—modify and change, as needed!"

Lesson 35: Solid Foundation (CONTINUED)

Discussion Questions and Prompts

1. We often say something has a purpose. What does that mean?

2. Can things have more than one purpose? Give an example.

3. What would you like to contribute to the world and others during your lifetime?

4. Why do you think businesses have purpose statements?

5. How can having an understanding or knowing your purpose benefit you?

6. How can one's purpose change or expand throughout life?

Solid Foundation-Purpose

Consider your purpose and complete the following prompts.

Write down things that you would like to contribute to the world.

_____

_____

On the picture above, write down things that you would like to contribute to others.

On the picture above, write other ideas you have about your purpose.

Using the ideas above, write a purpose statement for your life!

_____

Lesson 36: Just a Rock-Right?

Overview

Students will create a rock person while processing how everyone can contribute positively to the world and people around them.

Objectives

- Students will visually see examples of how each person is unique.
- Students will identify ways in which they can contribute positively to others.
- Students will create a rock person to serve as a reminder of how they can contribute to the world and others.

Materials

- Rocks
- Hot glue (if working with a large group, you may want to have more than one hot glue gun and an assistant to help with the glue)
- Markers or paint

Procedures

1. Instruct students to arrange rocks and create a person. Allow them to decorate using markers and paint (they can create clothes, eyes, hair, etc.). Hot glue the rocks together to form the person as each student finishes.
2. Allow students time to observe the rock people other students created. Highlight how although they are all rock people, none of them are the same. Ask students to point out some of the differences. Just as these rock people are all unique, so are we. We each have unique abilities and personalities. Share the following analogy, "Imagine a tree that is in full bloom with leaves. (If time/facilities permit, go outside and actually observe a tree). Each person can pick a leaf and they will all be unique. For some reason, in our world today we get a leaf and try to make others think it is the best leaf in the world. We criticize the other leaves and make sure we point out why the other ones are bad. But the truth is—all the leaves came from the same place—the tree. Don't you think we would be much better off if we just valued all the leaves?" Make application by pointing out this is what we often do to other people. We point out flaws, criticize, and condemn others. Each day, we have the opportunity to contribute

positively to the lives of others. Instead of choosing to point out flaws, criticize, and condemn, we could look for opportunities to encourage others, engage in random acts of kindness, and cheer others on.

3. Have students practice encouraging others and noticing positive things by allowing them to comment on other students' rock people. Point out that oftentimes in order to be in a position to notice the good in others, we must be aware of the good within ourselves. Instruct students to think about their lives. Allow students to discuss positive traits about themselves. Once every student has some ideas, allow him/her to write the traits on the rock person.

4. Now that students are aware of positive things about themselves, encourage them to brainstorm ways they can contribute positively in the lives of others. Guide them into being very specific. For example, instead of saying, "Helping others." Encourage them to identify how they can help, like "I can help my dad wash the car or I can help serve lunch on Saturdays at the homeless shelter."

Discussion Questions and Prompts

1. In what ways do you think you are unique?

_____

2. Tell about a time you may not have necessarily valued your "uniqueness."

_____

3. Share a time when someone pointed out your flaws, criticized, or condemned you for just being you.

_____

4. Share a time in which someone contributed positively to your life.

_____

5. In what ways can you contribute positively in the lives of others?

_____

Lesson 37: Making Sense of It

Overview

Students will create a thinking map that helps them explore the similarities and differences among their values and beliefs versus their peers.

Objectives

- Students will identify their core values and beliefs.
- Students will identify the perception of their peers' values and beliefs.
- Students will compare and contrast their ideals with their peers.

Materials

- Copy of *Making Sense of It* activity sheet for each student

Procedures

1. Begin with a discussion about how it is often difficult to make choices we feel are right when it seems that everyone around us may think those choices are uncool. We may want to pretend to have different values and beliefs or we may just act like we agree, when inside we really do not. In each of the situations, we are faced with conforming to the demands/beliefs of the group or going against the norm of the group. Going against the norm can be difficult. Just think how hard it would be to swim upstream. It takes much more effort than to just swim with the flow. Standing up to your peers and being yourself when the group seems to be much different, takes a strong person. Continue this discussion theme and allow students to offer input and examples.

2. Explain that one of the ways to be able to stand up and be yourself is to have a solid identity—really knowing who you are, what you believe, and what you stand for. Distribute copies of the Making Sense of It activity sheet. Explain the directions and encourage discussion as students process their values and beliefs. Allow them time to complete the activity.

3. Encourage students to share their responses highlighting things they learned or recognized during the activity. Ask them to share experiences when they have felt pressure to hide who they are in a group or with others. Begin a discussion and allow them to process ways they can stand up and be themselves without disrespecting others. Use some of the later discussion questions to get students to start discussing. Stress that just because beliefs/values are different among people does not mean they cannot get along or hang out. Discuss how people can be respectful of differences yet still be free to be themselves.

Discussion Questions and Prompts

1. Tell about a time you have hid your true feelings/thoughts because you knew all your peers would make fun of you for your ideals/beliefs.

   _____

2. How hard is it to really express who you are when you are in a group that has much different values/beliefs? Share an experience.

   _____

3. What values and beliefs are important to you?

   _____

4. What values and beliefs seem to be important to your peers?

   _____

5. How did you determine what values and beliefs seem important to your peers?

   _____

6. How do you demonstrate your values and beliefs?

   _____

7. How can you stand up and be yourself while at the same time respecting your peers?

   _____

8. Can you still associate and hang out with peers whose values/beliefs are different from yours?

   _____

9. What are the consequences of being yourself? What are the benefits of being yourself?

   _____

Making Sense of It

Think about the values and beliefs of you and your peers. In the bubbles connected to the peers rectangle, write values/beliefs you perceive they have that are different from yours. In the bubbles connected to the self rectangle, write your values and beliefs that are different from your peers. In the bubbles connected to both, write values/beliefs that you and your peers share.

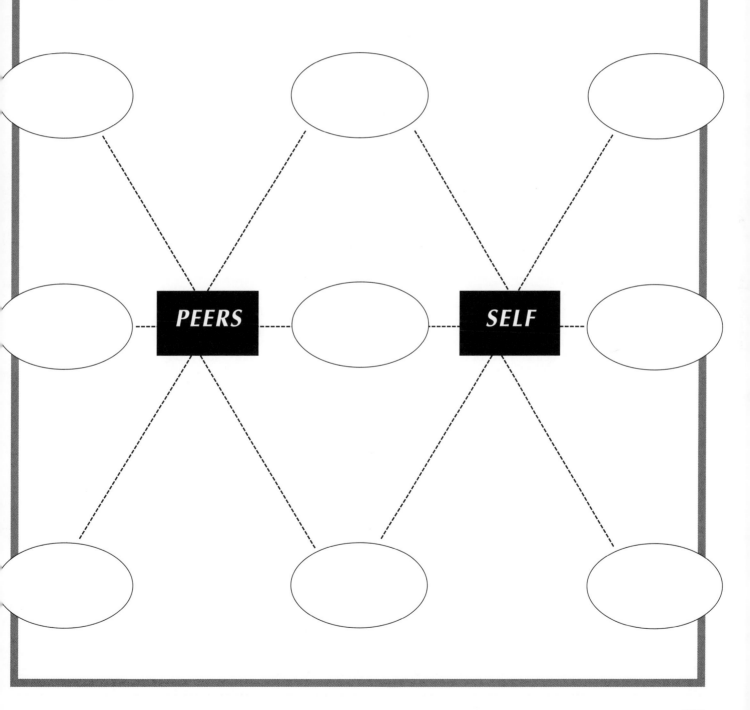

Lesson 38: Which One is the Best?

Overview

Students will process individual differences by exploring the characteristics of different types of slime.

Objectives

- Students will compare and contrast the properties of different types of slime.
- Students will discuss and debate which type of slime is "best."
- Students will understand that materials as well as people are different.
- Students will understand how individual differences are needed to accomplish different purposes.

Materials

- Slime recipes (make at least 2)

SLIME RECIPE #1

4 oz White glue (washable glues do not work as well)
1 1/2 cup of water
2 containers—bowls or cups

1 tsp Borax (found in store's laundry aisle)
Food coloring (optional)
2 stirring spoons

In one container, stir together 4 oz. of white glue with ½ cup water. *Optional—add food coloring to the mixture; Otherwise, it will be white.

In a separate container, mix 1 cup of water with 1 teaspoon of Borax.

Slowly, stir the glue recipe into the Borax mixture.

Pick up the slime that forms and knead with your hands until it feels dry. Discard the remaining water.

The more the slime is played with, the less sticky and firmer it will become.

Recipe copied from http://chemistry.about.com/cs/howtos/ht/slime.htm

---

SLIME RECIPE #2

2 parts glue
*Optional food coloring

1 part liquid starch-found in laundry detergent aisle

Mix ingredients until desired consistency. The longer you work with it, the better the consistency becomes.
Can be stored in an airtight container.
*Washable/school glues do not work as well; all purpose glues work best

---

Lesson 38: Which One is the Best?

(CONTINUED)

SLIME RECIPE #3

A container with warm water
1 tbsp. cornstarch
2 small containers/cups for mixing
Food coloring (optional)

1/2 tsp. of Borax
1 tbsp. glue
Craft stick/spoon for stirring

In one container, mix 2 tbsp. of warm water with 1/2 tsp Borax. If you want colored material, mix food coloring in. Stir until the Borax is dissolved. In the other container, put 1 tbsp. glue, 1/2 tsp. of the Borax mixture from the other container and 1 tbsp. of cornstarch. Without stirring, allow the mixture to sit for 10-15 seconds. Then, stir until it becomes impossible to stir. Take the mixture out and knead until it becomes rubbery.
(This slime mixture will bounce.)

Procedures

1. Allow students to make the slime according to the recipes. If time is an issue, you may want to have the slime made beforehand. Encourage students to play with the slime and explore the different properties. Ask them to identify some unique properties of each. Once they have manipulated it for a few minutes, allow them to compare and contrast the different slimes. If working in a group/classroom setting, divide students into groups and assign them a "slime." Have them debate using evidence which slime is "best." Afterwards, ask students, "Really, is one slime better than the other?" Discuss how each slime is different and actually just serves different purposes.

2. Make application by pointing out that as people we all have individual differences. These differences allow us to perform different tasks and make the world a richer place. For example: Some of the slime can bounce. Some of the other slime can not. Some people can paint or draw really well while others cannot. Imagine how life would be without paintings or drawings. On the other hand, what if everyone painted or drew well? Encourage students to discuss more examples, possibly using their own circumstances. If they are stuck, share some more ideas for talking points:
   • Introverts/Extroverts
   • Risk-takers/Safety-driven People
   • Organized/Unorganized
   • Jokesters/Serious

Lesson 38: Which One is the Best?

3. Lead into a discussion about the fact that we often look and admire other people's characteristics/abilities so much that we forget about our own. We feel that we do not have worth or that we do not have purpose. This is far from the truth. It is similar to us trying to argue which slime is best. The truth is that neither is the "best." They just have different properties. Encourage students to share/process some of their feelings regarding themselves and others. Share stories of people who did not seem to fit society's standard but found that the unique abilities they had eventually led to the fulfillment of great life accomplishments. (For example: Einstein, William Carey, Elvis Presley, etc.) Sometimes, the very things that we are picked on or made fun of about turn out to be our most valuable qualities later in life!

Discussion Questions and Prompts

1. What are your properties (characteristics/traits) that make you unique?

   _____

   _____

2. Share a time in which you felt like your traits or abilities were not as valued as someone else's.

   _____

   _____

3. What are the benefits to us all having unique characteristics?

   _____

   _____

4. Explain how a person's individual uniqueness can contribute to his/her specific purpose.

   _____

   _____

Lesson 39: What is More Important?

Overview

Students will decorate a cup as character traits and outside appearances are processed.

Objectives

- Students will process and understand the difference between outward and inward characteristics of themselves.
- Students will see a visual example of how the outside can look appealing but the inside can be very unappealing.
- Students will identify the inward characteristics they desire to possess.

Materials

- A cup that looks fine on the outside but is filthy on the inside
- A cup for each student (styrofoam, paper, plastic, etc.)
- Permanent markers or paint
- Any other embellishments you may chose for the cup
- Strips of paper

Procedures

1. Show the students only the outside of the dirty cup. Ask them if the cup is suitable for drinking. Ask them to explain why they think the cup is suitable for drinking. Once students discuss this, show them the inside of the cup and ask if they have a different opinion about the cup now. For some reason, in our society, we tend to make lots of judgements/decisions based on the information we see on the outside. People make judgements about the quality of books based on the cover. We make judgments about how reliable vehicles are by the way they look. We make judgments about people based on their outward appearance. Encourage students to share their experiences.
2. Prompt a discussion regarding the difference between outward and inward characteristics. If students feel comfortable encourage them to share. If not, move on to the next procedure.

Lesson 39: What is More Important?

(CONTINUED)

3. Distribute cups to all the students. Instruct them to decorate the cups any way they choose. Afterwards, distribute strips of paper and allow students to write down inward characteristics they want to possess/demonstrate with their life. As students share these traits, encourage them to discuss what the evidence of these traits are within one's life. For example, one may share they want to be compassionate. Compassion is demonstrated by serving others, doing acts of kindness, and taking the time out to really listen to the needs of others.

Discussion Questions and Prompts

1. How can making judgments based on the outward appearance of something or someone be deceiving?

2. Share a time you have made a misjudgment based on the outward appearance of something.

3. How does it feel when people judge you based on your outward characteristics?

4. What is the difference between inward and outward characteristics?

5. What inward characteristics do you want to possess?

6. What do these inward characteristics "look" like? What is the evidence that one possesses these traits?

Lesson 40: A Collage of Me

Overview

Students create a symbol collage that represents one's uniqueness and fosters appreciation of individual differences.

Objectives

- Students will make an artistic representation of their uniqueness.
- Students will learn how to use the art to remind themselves of how appreciating their uniqueness can lead to a more solid identity.

Materials

- Dough recipe (page 16)
- Paint
- Paper/newspaper to lay under objects when painting
- Glue

Procedures

1. Review previous session material regarding uniqueness and identity. Encourage students to share their thoughts/ideas about their individual uniqueness. Ask a student to share one or more of their traits. After they share, ask how they would visually represent that trait with a symbol. Explain that during today's activity they are going to visually represent their identity using symbols for their uniqueness.

2. Give students a portion of the dough. Instruct them to make a base for the art. Explain they may want to create a round base like a medallion or a small box or some other shape. All of the symbols will be attached to this base. After the base is created, allow them to create symbols for the traits they identify. It may help if they list the traits on paper before they begin making the symbols. They should take the symbols and place them on the base. They may want to add some glue if they do not think the dough will adhere once it dries. Allow students to paint the creation. Allow the dough to air dry for a week. If you want, this can be broken up into 2 sessions. During the first, the base and symbols can be made. During the 2nd session, (once the things have hardened/dried) they can be painted.

Lesson 40: A Collage of Me

(CONTINUED)

3. Once completed, explain that sometimes during the course of life we get discouraged and forget that who we are really does matter. We may feel we do not do things as well as everyone around us or that no one really notices our efforts. In those times of discouragement, this art piece can serve as a reminder that you do have a purpose. When searching for or exploring your identity these symbols can be a starting place to help you to understand who you are and what your purpose may be.

Discussion Questions and Prompts

1. Share any additional thoughts about your identity and/or uniqueness you have had since we have been discussing these things.

_____

_____

2. List the traits that make up your uniqueness/identity.

_____

_____

3. How can this art piece be an encouragement to you?

_____

_____

Lesson 41: Blended Beauty

Overview

Students will create a melted crayon mosaic as they process the concept of synergy.

Objectives

- Students will be able to define the term synergy.
- Students will understand that while we are all unique and different, we should still make an effort to effectively work with others.
- Students will see how a group project is greater than all the individual pieces.

Materials

- Wax paper
- Scissors
- Crayons
- Crayon sharpener for shaving crayons
- Iron

Procedures

1. Begin a discussion about how everyone has individual differences, but when those differences work together, a beautiful product often emerges. For example, one person may be a great writer but a poor artist. When the author works with an artist/illustrator, a book can be completed. While both are good on their own, the written work and the art put together make an even better product. The process of combining two or more things, agents, substances, or works to create a greater combined effort or product is called synergy. The finished product is greater than the individual parts. Encourage students to share examples (singer/band; a person with an idea/a person with the ability to make the idea happen, etc.). Point out that often our differences/uniqueness interact with others and can make working together a little challenging. Encourage students to share their experiences working with other people. Explain that while working with others can have some frustrating aspects, when all parts are contributing and allowed to express themselves fully, a better product results.

2. Ask each student to select a crayon that is his/her favorite color from the selection you have. Plug the iron in and allow it to be heating on low-medium heat. Allow students to sharpen the crayon over the wax paper. Allow the shavings to fall onto the paper. Once all students have contributed shavings, take another piece of wax paper and place it on top of the shavings, wax-side down. Iron the two pieces together until the shavings have melted and blended together. Show the group the completed result. Now, quickly repeat the process using two smaller pieces of wax paper. Only use shavings from one crayon. Show students the differences between the group project and the individual project. Use the visual as an additional talking point about combining our uniqueness into a group productto create synergy. Have the students continue the discussion regarding the concepts using the following questions and prompts.

Discussion Questions and Prompts

1. What is synergy? Give an example.

_____

2. Share an experience in which you have felt your idea was better than someone else's and because of that it kept you from working with others.

_____

3. What are the difficulties that arise when working with others? What are the benefits to working with others?

_____

4. What are the difficulties and benefits to working alone?

_____

5. While it is important for us to know who we are and how we are unique to form a more healthy identity, how can we benefit from valuing others' uniqueness as well?

_____

Lesson 42: If I Waved a Wand...

Overview

Students will engage in solution focus therapy techniques as they deal with issues such as being bullied, change, self-esteem, differences, identity, and/or goals as they create magic wands.
**Note: This session is easily adapted to address a multitude of issues. However, this written session will only address identity issues in regards to one's future.*

Objectives

- Students will begin processing their thoughts about the future.
- Students will answer a form of miracle question in regards to their future.
- Students will identify coping strategies they have used to overcome obstacles in their lives.
- Students will give specific examples of how they can be the magic in regards to their own future.

Materials

- Material for making wands (options: cardboard, cardstock, foam sheets, dowel rods, paper that they can roll, etc.)
- Markers or paint for decorating
- Scissors
- Any additional embellishments (ribbon, glitter, colored tape, etc.)
- Copy of **Waved Wand** activity sheet for each student (in lieu of cardboard creation activity)
- A magic wand (one created prior to the session or a purchased one)

Procedures

1. Begin a discussion by explaining to students that people often think counselors are like magic wands. They believe that they can go see a counselor, a counselor will do something magical, and the next day they will be all better. The truth is, while a counselor can be a facilitator of change, the person themselves are responsible for the change in their own lives. Explain that during today's session, they are going to process their thoughts and feelings regarding their future. Explain that having a healthy identity includes knowing, accepting, and understanding one's self. In addition, he/she finds how to successfully appreciate the differences of others and forms a positive outlook regarding his/her future. Wave your magic wands and say, "If it

were up to me, I would wave this wand and you all would leave here with a positive view about your future! Now, let's get to work and see how well my wand works!"

2. Allow students to spend a few minutes discussing what they envision regarding their future (next year, five years, 20 years, etc.). Instruct students to pick one of the things they listed/discussed to explore further. For example, someone may have said they want to be a cosmetologist. Once they have identified what they want to explore further, ask a form of the miracle question: "Tonight you go to bed and a miracle happens. What you envisioned has happened. When you wake up tomorrow what will be the evidence that the miracle has occurred?" Encourage discussion/feedback. If students verbalize obstacles to achieving their desired future, allow them to process it by asking how they have overcome similar obstacles in the past. Use students' responses as additional discussion points.

3. If using the activity sheet instead of creating wands, distribute copies of **Waved Wand** and allow students to complete the activity. If creating wands, distribute the material and decorating supplies. Instruct them to create magic wands. Ask students to write, somewhere on their wands, "I can be the magic." Once created or when the activity sheet is complete, explain that as their life continues, they will be the agent that greatly determines the direction of their future. Offer some encouragement and motivation by pointing out positive characteristics of the students. Allow students to discuss how they can be the magic in regards to their future (make goal-oriented choices, engage in certain actions, etc.). Allow students to take the wands home as a visual reminder of the session.

Discussion Questions and Prompts

1. If you had a working magic wand, what would you do with it?

_____

2. When you think about your future, what are your thoughts?

_____

3. If you foresee any obstacles to achieving your desired future, discuss how you have overcome similar obstacles in the past.

_____

4. How can you be the magic in regards to your future? Share specific examples.

_____

Waved Wand

Decorate the magic wand of your choice.

Lesson 43: Go Out on a Limb

Overview

Students will create a bottle mobile containing short and long goals.

Objectives

- Students will understand the process of goal setting.
- Students will be introduced to William Glasser's WDEP concept.
- Student will identify what they "want" and set long term and short term goals.

Materials

- Random pictures or clip art that can serve as talking points for goal setting (pictures of any type of sport activities, a high school diploma/graduation, driver's license, etc.)
- Plastic bottle(s)
- ** *Note: Several modifications are possible. You may chose to use 1 bottle for the entire group; one bottle per student; or several bottles per student.*
- A branch for tying the bottles on (if facilities permit, you may choose to hang the mobile outside on a live tree)
- Yarn/string
- Permanent markers, paint, paper, glue (any items to help in decorating the bottles)
- Strip of paper
- Copy of **WDEP** activity sheet for each student

Procedures

1. Begin with a general discussion about goals and goal setting. Use the pictures and/or clip art as discussion starters. For example, show a picture of a driver's license. State that one may have a goal of getting his/her license. Have students discuss what it takes to actually achieve the goal of getting the license (studying/passing a written test, practicing driving skills, passing a driving test, etc.). Once they identify what is needed to achieve the goal, encourage them to break it down further by specifically identifying actions that are needed to achieve the goal. For example: What actions are necessary to pass the written/computer-based test? You must study the driver's manual, local driving laws, road signage, take practice tests, etc.

2. Introduce William Glasser's WDEP technique (Glasser, 2010). W–What do you want? D–What are you doing to gain/accomplish what you want? E–Evaluate how well what you are

doing is working to get what you want? P–Adjust your plan/actions to help you get closer to your goal. Highlight that having direction and knowing what you want to accomplish and/or gain in life helps keep you going in a positive direction. For example: If you want to be a professional sports player, you must have grades sufficient enough to go to college. Therefore, when you are tempted not to do your best, your desire to be a sports player may be the motivation necessary to keep yourself disciplined and working toward your goal. Allow students to discuss/process this concept.

3. Once the students demonstrate understanding of the WDEP process, allow them to begin working through the process–identifying what they want, what they are doing, etc. using the **WDEP** activity sheet. Encourage students to share their insights regarding goals and behavior.

4. Instruct students to write their goals on strips of paper. Explain that in order to reach goals, sometimes we have to break a large goal into smaller steps/goals. For example: Your goal may be to graduate high school. However, a shorter-term goal to achieving that may be to pass 10th grade. Even shorter term than that, you may need to pass an upcoming unit test. Ask students to look at the goal they wrote on the strip of paper. Give students an additional strip or two and have them write down short term goals that will help them achieve the long term goal. Once goals are identified, allow students to place the strips of paper (goals) in the bottle(s). If using one bottle for the group, allow them to put them all in the bottle. If using multiple bottles, you may choose to have a bottle for short term goals and one for long term goals. Allow students to decorate the bottle(s). Once decorated, tie the bottle(s) onto the limb to display in the room or hang from a tree outside.

Discussion Questions and Prompts

1. What is a goal?

2. How are goals achieved?

3. What is the difference between short term and long term goals?

4. How can setting goals and working to achieve them help you build a more solid identity?

5. What are some goals that you would like to achieve?

6. What are some short term goals you would need to achieve in order to achieve the long term goal?

WDEP

W –What do you want?

_____

_____

_____

D –What are you doing to gain what you want?

_____

_____

_____

E –How is it working? (How are your actions helping you achieve what you want?)

_____

_____

P –What do you need to do regarding your plan? (Continue with current path or make changes?)

_____

_____

Lesson 44: Swimming Upstream

Overview

Students will create a fish as they process the pressures and challenges of not giving in to peer pressure.

Objectives

- Students will verbalize the difficulties of standing up to peer pressure.
- Students will process what actions are necessary to resist giving into pressure.
- Students will outline a plan they can follow the next time they have to "swim upstream" (withstand peer pressure).

Materials

- Colored paper, tissue paper, paper plates (any paper materials that can be used to create a fish)
- Glue
- Scissors
- Markers

Procedures

1. Open with a discussion about peer pressure. Use the analogy of trying to swim upstream or against a current when discussing the concept. For example, when you are swimming with the current, it is pretty easy. However, when you try to swim against the current, the process of swimming becomes much more difficult. The force of the water is pushing against you. The same is true when you are trying to make a decision/choice. As long as everyone agrees with your choice it is not that difficult. However, if you go against what the majority is doing, all of a sudden you feel pressure. How would you describe the "pressure" felt when trying to resist peer pressure? Encourage students to process/discuss why they feel pressure from peers?

(CONTINUED)

2. Instruct students to use the available crafting materials to construct a fish. When they are finished, begin a discussion about the skills, traits, and/or actions they think are necessary to withstand peer pressure. Once they have brainstormed many ideas, encourage students to think about their own situations—times they have successfully withstood peer pressure and times they have given into pressure. Using the ideas brainstormed, ask them to write strategies, actions and traits on their fish that they think will be useful the next time they are facing peer pressure.

3. Explain that one of the best strategies to withstand peer pressure is having a solid identity. Part of forming an identity includes knowing yourself, what you want, and what you need to do to achieve what you want. Making decisions that align with these ideals can help you withstand the pressure to engage in actions that go against them. The next time you find yourself trying to swim upstream use this fish as an encouragement for you to have the strength to stand for your ideals.

Discussion Questions and Prompts

1. Share a time that you have experienced peer pressure.

_____

_____

2. What are the possible negative and positive effects of not going along with the crowd?

_____

_____

3. Why do you think we sometimes feel pressure to conform to our peers?

_____

_____

4. What strategies do you think are successful to use when trying to swim upstream (go against peer pressure)?

_____

_____

References

Brafman, R. (2011). *Succeeding when you're suppose to fail.* New York, NY: Random House, Inc.

Gladding, S. (2011). *The creative arts in counseling.* Alexandria, VA: American School Counselor Association.

Glasser, W. (2010). *Choice theory: a new psychology of personal freedom.* New York, NY: Harper Collins.

Schimmel, C. (2006/2007). Seeing is remembering: the impact of using creative props with children in schools and community agencies. *Journal of Creativity in Mental Heatlh*, 2, 59-74.

Waliski, A. (2009). An introduction to expressive and creative techniques for counselors in training. *Journal of Creativity and Mental Health*, 4, 375-385.

About the Author

Paula Cox has worked as a counselor for the past fifteen years in mental health, school, and private practice settings. Currently, she is an Adjunct Professor within the Counselor Education Program at the University of Mississippi and provides supervision for counselors seeking LPC licensure. She also speaks several times a year at counseling related conferences. Her current full-time work includes being mom and a home-school teacher for her two energetic boys. She has been married to her husband for almost eighteen years, and they currently reside in Blue Springs, MS. She earned her Ph.D. from the University of MS. She is the co-author of another YouthLight publication, *Therapeutic Interventions using Non-therapeutic Games.* Paula's overall mission as a person and professional is to help others seek to live a meaningful life!

Live a Meaningful Life!